From Can't See to Can't See

HOW THE CHAINS OF LABOR AND LACK STILL BIND US , FROM THE CAROLINAS TO THE CARIBBEAN

DR. CASSIUS V. STUART
&
DR. SHARMAINE STUART

From Can't See to Can't See

HOW THE CHAINS OF LABOR AND LACK STILL BIND US, FROM THE CAROLINAS TO THE CARIBBEAN

Dr. CASSIUS V. STUART
Dr. SHARMAINE STUART

Printed Worldwide
First Printing 2026
First Edition 2026

9798989636877

From Can’t See to Can’t See

HOW THE CHAINS OF LABOR AND LACK STILL BIND US, FROM THE CAROLINAS TO THE CARIBBEAN

DEDICATION

To the ancestors who labored from can't see to can't see
whose sweat watered the soil of survival,
whose voices broke through chains,
and whose dreams became the blueprint of our inheritance.
To our family past, present, and yet to come,
you remain our reason, our anchor, and our unshakable hope.
And to all who still rise against the weight of history, this
book is for you.
May you **possess the land wherever you are.**

Acknowledgments

This work is the fruit of more than our own hands; it is the echo of many voices, the strength of a community, and the wisdom of generations.

First, we thank God, the ultimate author of freedom, for carrying us through every trial and for reminding us that liberation is not only possible but promised.

To our parents and elders, you instilled in us discipline, faith, and a love for the truth. Your sacrifices watered the soil from which these words have grown.

To our children and loved ones, you remind us daily why the struggle for dignity and justice must never end. Your laughter, questions, and hope are the compass that keeps us moving forward.

To Shonalee Munroe, without whom this book would not have been possible, your encouragement, insight, and presence have been a vital part of this journey.

To our teachers, colleagues, and friends who challenged our ideas, sharpened our vision, and refused to let us settle for less than excellence, we are forever grateful.

To the Bahamian people, to the Caribbean diaspora, and to our ancestors in the United States, particularly the Gullah-Geechee communities and to all who have labored in the shadows yet shine with resilience: this book carries your story, your memory, and your fire.

And finally, to you, the reader: may these pages awaken memory, stir courage, and inspire action. May you find in them not just words, but a blueprint for freedom that we are all called to build together.

FOREWORD

From Can't See to Can't See is more than a history book; it is a challenge to examine whether freedom without ownership is truly freedom at all.

In this thought-provoking work, Dr. Cassius Stuart and Dr. Sharmaine Stuart connect the struggles of enslaved Africans in the Carolinas and the Caribbean to many of the economic realities that persist today. Through history, culture, and social analysis, they invite readers to consider how systems of labor, poverty, and dependency continue to shape communities generations after emancipation.

What makes this book significant is its refusal to stop at the problem. The authors call us to think beyond survival and toward ownership, legacy, opportunity, and generational advancement. They remind us that true liberation is not simply the breaking of chains, but the creation of pathways that allow people to thrive.

Whether you read this book as history, social commentary, or a call to action, it will leave you reflecting on the relationship between work, freedom, and the future we hope to build for the next generation.

I commend the authors for tackling an important and often uncomfortable subject with courage and conviction. May these pages inspire meaningful dialogue, deeper understanding, and renewed commitment to building communities where freedom is measured not only by what we have escaped, but by what we are able to create.

Dr. Donald McCartney

TABLE OF CONTENTS

CONTENTS

PREFACE

"I don't believe freedom is just about being unchained, real freedom means ownership. Ownership of land. Ownership of businesses. Ownership of the power to determine your own future, not just for you, but for your children, and your children's children. And that's the kind of freedom Black people in the South and the Caribbean have never truly had."

— ***Cassius Stuart***

"We can free thousands from poverty, if only they knew they were still bound. But many are blinded by survival, addicted to the grind, and convinced that struggle is normal. Until they see, they won't follow the way out."

— ***Cassius Stuart***

These words are not just reflections; they are a charge. For too long, the labor of Black communities, whether in the rice fields of the Carolinas or the sugar estates of the Caribbean, was stolen from dawn to dusk, "from can't see to can't see," leaving little more than survival. The chains may have fallen, but the grind remains, rebranded through poverty, low wages, and systems that demand work without legacy.

This book is born out of that truth: that survival is not enough. Our people deserve more than exhaustion. We deserve rest, ownership, vision, and the structures that turn fleeting freedom into generational power. Like Harriet Tubman's Underground Railroad, this journey is not about escape alone; it's about going back, building pathways, and ensuring no one is left behind.

The chapters that follow weave history, theology, economics, and lived experience into a blueprint. From Sabbath rest to cooperative economics, from "each one help one" to global lessons drawn from Jewish, Asian, and even state-backed diaspora strategies, this book insists that freedom is not inherited, it is structured.

This preface, therefore, is not an introduction but an invitation. An invitation to see beyond survival. An invitation to build legacies that last. An invitation to transform "can't see" into vision, ownership, and liberation.

Because true freedom does not begin in the grind, it begins in the pause. It takes root in land and business. And it blossoms when we dare to build together, so that our children and their children inherit not chains, but choices.

INTRODUCTION: STILL IN THE FIELDS

From Can't See to Can't See: How the Chains of Labor and Lack Still Bind Us, From the Carolinas to the Caribbean

There's a phrase etched like a scar across the memory of Black America: ***"From can't see to can't see."***

It was not just a saying, it was survival's rhythm. It meant rising before the sun, in darkness so thick you could not see your own hand, and working until the night reclaimed the sky, when you could not see again. It meant laboring under overseers whose whips, not clocks, measured the hours. It meant losing not just freedom, but time itself, time to rest, time to imagine, time to love, time to be human.

What haunts us is that centuries later, the echo lingers.

Walk through the streets of Charleston, where rice once built fortunes for everyone but the hands that planted it. Stand on the porches of Nassau, where colonial hierarchies still shape opportunity. Listen in Kingston's crowded markets, Haiti's battered hills, or Port of Spain's restless crossroads. You'll hear it still: the grind.

We still grind but we cannot see. We cannot see rest.

We cannot see peace.

We cannot see freedom beyond survival.

We cannot see the invisible chains even as we swear we've been freed.

And this blindness is its own bondage. For though the chains of iron were broken, the chains of exhaustion, poverty, and survival remain. The plantation clock may be gone, but the system it birthed, capitalism rooted in stolen labor still ticks inside us.

This book begins here: with the haunting truth that we are still in the fields. Some fields are literal, bent back in agriculture and tourism; others are figurative office cubicles, gig apps, low-wage jobs, endless hustle. But all demand the same thing: labor without legacy. Work without ownership. Grind without growth.

The question before us is this: how do we break free when the fields look different, but the hours remain the same? How do we reclaim what was stolen-not just freedom from chains, but freedom of time, rest, vision, and inheritance?

This introduction is not a lament it is a call to action. A call to see clearly what has been hiding in plain sight. A call to name the grind for what it is: a theft of life. And a call to imagine what our ancestors dreamed in the dark: not endless labor, but liberation that endures.

THE ROOTS: DEFINING "FROM CAN'T SEE TO CAN'T SEE"

They dangled promises: 40 acres and a mule, land to rebuild on, reparations to heal. But the promise was a mirage. Instead, sharecropping bound our people in endless debt. Redlining locked us out of homes and neighborhoods. Minimum-wage traps kept our bellies empty while our hands stayed calloused. In the Caribbean, "freedom" came hollow no land, no tools, just fields that still demanded tending by broken hands: the sugar estates of Jamaica, the coffee hills of Haiti, the oil fields of Trinidad.

We're not picking cotton anymore, but the soil clings to us. The weight we carry now is not from masters with whips, but from systems with policies. Survival has replaced thriving. Exhaustion is mistaken for strength. Suffering is glorified as pride. And so, we hustle till it hollows us, then pass the toil to our children like an heirloom curse.

Let me be clear:
If you labor endlessly and still fall short, you are not free.
If your children inherit your starting line, you are not free.
If you do not own your time, your land, your legacy you are not free.

The phrase ***"from can't see to can't see"*** was born in the antebellum South, before emancipation's hollow dawn. Cabins stirred in dew-soaked dread as enslaved men, women, and children rose from dirt floors to face another day of endless toil. No bells rang; whips cracked. They worked from the moment their hands disappeared into the darkness of pre-dawn until the stars reclaimed the sky. They harvested, planted, bled, and endured under the sun's indifferent gaze.

No wages. No mercy. Just a system engineered to shatter bodies and strip souls. And yet, amid the agony, they forged words a code whispered in the shadows: ***"I am weary. I am exploited. I endure. But I see the truth."***

That shorthand survived emancipation, carried like a scar across generations. From South Carolina rice fields to Mississippi porches, it echoed in barbershops, churches, kitchens, and break rooms. And today, it still resonates among janitors, nurses, drivers, farmhands, warehouse workers, those who rise before dawn and return long after dusk, not by choice, but by necessity.

One job? Not enough. Rent devours paychecks. Groceries shrink while bills multiply. The system remains rigged.

The fields have morphed: overseers wear suits, whips disguise themselves as policies, cabins have become cramped apartments, and cotton has given way to clock-ins and gig work. But the exhaustion? Poverty? The stasis? Unchanged.

Whether in Charleston or Compton, Nassau or Kingston, Port-au-Prince or New York, we still rise in darkness, chasing scraps. Still can't see the exit. Still can't see ownership. Still can't see legacy.

This is not laziness it is centuries of burden piled on weary shoulders. We cried for 40 acres and a mule. Today, that cry evolves: ***"Give us ground to build. Let us own. Let us breathe."***

Why This Book? A Wake-Up and a Roadmap

This isn't just history, it's a reckoning. A mirror held up to expose systems that were never dismantled, only redesigned, polished, and repackaged to look like progress. From the rice fields of the Carolinas to the sugar estates of Jamaica, from Haiti's mountains scarred by revolution's betrayal to Trinidad's oil fields feeding foreign wealth, the pattern is the same: Black bodies labor, yet the fruits of that labor rarely belong to us.

This book serves as a bridge between the past and the present, illustrating how the shackles of yesterday have become the economic traps of today low wages, land loss, debt cycles, tourism dependency, and foreign ownership. It is here to shatter myths that keep us bound that hustle is holiness, that exhaustion is strength, that mere survival counts as success. Survival may keep us breathing, but it does not set us free.

We will name the patterns that others prefer to leave unspoken: how policies masquerade as progress while stripping opportunities, how poverty is framed as personal failure instead of systemic theft, and how often our communities are convinced to celebrate scraps as though they were banquets. We will break the silence that comforts oppressors but suffocates the oppressed.

Most of all, this is a roadmap. Not toward fleeting escape, but toward rooted liberation, ownership of land, ownership of businesses, ownership of time, and ownership of destinies. Not only for us, but for our children, and their children, and the generations we will never meet but who will inherit the world we build.

We have labored in darkness long enough. It is time to lift our eyes, see clearly, and claim what is rightfully ours. From here, we do not simply toil in the fields. From here, we lead the exodus, out of survival, into sovereignty; out of grinding, into growing; out of blindness, into vision.

"This labor was never a choice, but a mandate for survival under terror enforced by the whip, the auction block, and the ever-present shadow of death, turning human endurance into a weapon against itself."

PART ONE

ROOTS IN THE SOUTHERN SOIL

Chapter 1

THE PHRASE THAT SPEAKS VOLUMES

In the shadowed annals of Black history, certain words carry the weight of chains. "From can't see to can't see" is one such phrase a stark, unflinching testament to the brutality of enslaved life. It was not coined by scholars or preachers, but born from the weary lips of those whose bodies bore the scars of the lash. It speaks of stolen time, of days that stretched beyond the horizon, when the sun's rise and fall did not mark nature's rhythm but the boundaries of human endurance. It whispers of lives devoured by labor, where rest was stolen, dreams deferred, and humanity denied.

Origin of the Term Among Enslaved Africans

The phrase ***"from can't see to can't see"*** traces its roots directly to the rice and cotton plantations of the antebellum South. Enslaved Africans kidnapped from their homelands and thrust into America's chattel system, coined it to describe the relentless toil that consumed every ounce of light. Emerging in places like South Carolina's Lowcountry, Savannah, Georgia, and Jacksonville, Florida, where rice, cotton, and sugar fueled the young nation's economy, it captured a life where visibility itself marked labor's cruel boundaries.

Rising at 4 or 5 a.m., often roused by the crack of the overseer's whip, men, women, and children shuffled into the fields while the world was still cloaked in darkness, so dim they literally "can't see" their own hands. The day unfolded in grueling monotony: planting, hoping, harvesting under merciless heat, with meager meals and rare breaks. Punishment was swift for even the smallest act of resistance. And only when dusk swallowed the horizon, when sight once again vanished into night, did the work relent. By then, bodies were broken yet tomorrow promised the same. Twelve, fourteen, even sixteen-hour days became the normal cycle not of survival, but of engineered destruction.

This wasn't mere folklore. It is recorded in plantation journals, whispered in slave narratives, and preserved in songs of lament. In South Carolina's Gullah-Geechee communities, descendants recall how the phrase tied labor to suffering, its cadence echoing African linguistic roots twisted to fit New World chains. And the saying was not confined to the American South it reverberated across the Caribbean. On Jamaica's sugar plantations, Haiti's coffee slopes, and Barbados' cane fields, enslaved Africans endured the same dawn-to-dusk work, their days measured not in hours but in exhaustion. The phrase became a transatlantic code of bondage, a shared lexicon of pain across the Black diaspora.

Cultural Meaning in Oral Tradition

Beyond its literal description, ***"from can't see to can't see"*** carried profound cultural resonance. It was not only a phrase of survival but also a vessel of memory, woven into the fabric of oral tradition that sustained enslaved communities. In a world where literacy was often forbidden, where books and records were wielded as tools of control by the oppressor, words became weapons, sharp, coded, and enduring. Through whispers, chants, and spirituals, language itself became a secret resistance, preserving truth when written history sought to erase it.

The phrase was shorthand for collective pain and shared endurance: "I am weary, but I endure. I am bound, but I see." It echoed through folktales, in spirituals sung in the hush of night, and in murmurs exchanged on the porches of slave cabins. Grandmothers whispered it as warnings and lessons to children, embedding it in their memory as both caution and strength. Preachers thundered it in sermons, twisting its despair into defiance, linking individual hardship to communal survival. Even after emancipation, it lingered on Black porches, in barbershops, in church testimonies, and at Juneteenth gatherings less a phrase of oppression than a badge of resilience and remembrance.

This oral transmission was vital. It transformed suffering into a legacy and a legacy into instruction. Like African proverbs carried across the Middle Passage, the phrase was layered with irony and subversion. It mocked the enslavers' blindness to Black humanity while affirming the enslaver's clarity of injustice. It reminded the community that although the oppressor controlled the clock, they did not own the spirit.

In the Caribbean, parallel expressions in Creole and patois carried the same weight. On Jamaican sugar estates, in Haitian coffee hills, or among Trinidadian cane cutters, phrases describing "sunrise-to-sunset" toil held equal power, woven into songs and tales of marronage (escape). These

Stories fused endless labor with the dream of freedom, embedding hope in oral tradition. The continuity across the Carolinas and the Caribbean forged a pan-African cultural thread: no matter the soil or the overseer, the cry of ***"can't see to can't see"*** was a shared code a rhythm of survival, a chronicle of injustice, and a declaration of unbroken spirit.

Labor from Before Sunrise to After Dark as Survival, Not Choice

At its core, ***"from can't see to can't see"*** lays bare a fundamental truth: this labor was never a choice it was survival under terror. Enslaved Africans did not select their hours; the system carved them in blood and fear, enforced by overseers' whips, auction blocks, and the ever-present threat of death. From the moment cabin doors creaked open in the predawn dark, the day's grind was inescapable. Labor was not an occupation; it was a sentence.

Survival meant bending without breaking. Women worked while pregnant, giving birth in fields and returning days later, babies strapped to their backs. Children as young as five or six joined the lines, hands raw from cotton or cane. Elders were driven until collapse, their bodies discarded when deemed "unproductive." This was not just physical exhaustion, it was psychological warfare designed to erode identity, discipline spirit, and turn human beings into instruments of profit.

Yet, even within this forced rhythm, subversion found cracks. Feet slowed to a syncopated pace that mocked the overseer's commands. Songs rose across fields, spirituals that seemed harmless hymns but carried hidden messages of defiance and escape. Some stole moments of stolen rest, leaning on hoes or pausing at water breaks, defying the machine by claiming seconds of dignity. Even after dark, when the workday ended, "can't see" did not mean freedom. It meant different labor: patching clothes, tending small garden plots, nursing the sick, or soothing children by the light of fireflies. Exhaustion was relentless, but the community survived in those midnight hours.

This was never an ambition. Never hustle. It was existence on the edge, where life was reduced to cycles of labor without end. After emancipation, the phrase persisted because its reality continued to exist. Sharecropping chained families to fields under crushing debt. Convict leasing in the Carolinas and beyond recreated slavery in prison camps where Black men worked under gun and whip. In the Caribbean, "independence" often arrived hollow, leaving workers landless on the very plantations where their ancestors bled, grinding from dawn to dusk for meager wages controlled by foreign owners.

And today, the echo is still with us. It lives in low-wage jobs across the diaspora, where Black and Caribbean workers pull double shifts in warehouses, hospitals, and hotels, scraping for survival while wealth flows upward. It lives in the endless hustle glorified as strength, even as it hollows us out. It lives wherever survival still demands endless hours, proving that true choice remains elusive.

The phrase refuses to be silent because it is more than history it is testimony. It demands that we listen. It demands we act. It demands we imagine a future where labor is not a weapon of oppression, but a tool for building legacy, dignity, and abundance.

What made this labor even more devastating was the way it stole not just hours, but imagination. In a regime demanding constant output, rest itself became a threat. Enslaved people were denied the mental space to dream, to plan, or to envision futures beyond the fields. This theft of possibility was deliberate: a people too exhausted to think are a people too exhausted to resist. Yet despite this, flashes of creativity still survived.

The night hours those brief moments after overseers withdrew became an underground economy of survival. Men repaired broken tools from scraps; women created medicines from roots and leaves; elders preserved African memory through proverbs, rhythms, and origin stories. These acts were forms of cultural refusal,the rebuilding of identities plantation owners believed they had erased. In those fragile, flickering moments, a different kind of work began: the labor of holding on to selfhood.

In many ways, the modern world has refined what the plantation started. The tools have changed shift work, gig apps, stagnant wages, rising costs but the effect feels familiar. Time, once stolen by overseers, is now consumed by economic pressure. People work through nights, stretching themselves thin to survive systems designed to keep them behind. The whip has been replaced by rent, bills, and inflation, yet the demand remains: work until darkness takes you, rise before dawn, and repeat.

What the ancestors endured was not only long hours it was the intentional destruction of rest. And rest is not luxury; it is resistance. Rest is the ground where thought, community, and future-building take root. Without it, people stay trapped in survival mode, unable to imagine or pursue liberation.

Their endurance calls us to reclaim what was stolen not only land or wages, but time itself. Because the true legacy of "from can't see to can't see" is not only suffering, but the determination to build a world where worth is not measured by exhaustion; where labor sustains rather than consumes; and where rest becomes a birthright, not a battle.

Chapter 2

SLAVERY IN THE CAROLINAS

The Carolinas, North and South stood as crucibles of colonial ambition, where fertile soil and swampy low-country marshes gave birth not just to crops, but to an empire built on human bondage. Charleston, Georgetown, and the coastal plantations became engines of wealth for the colonial elite, exporting rice, indigo, and cotton to Europe and the wider Atlantic world. But this prosperity was not the fruit of innovation, it was the harvest of suffering.

Here, slavery was not an afterthought. It was a meticulously engineered machine of exploitation, calibrated to extract the maximum from enslaved Africans while offering the minimum chance of survival. Rice cultivation demanded relentless, backbreaking labor in waterlogged fields swarming with mosquitoes, where malaria and dysentery claimed lives as quickly as whips and overseers did. Indigo vats stained both fabric and flesh, their toxic fumes destroying lungs and skin. The wealth that built Charleston's stately homes and crowned its elites as colonial aristocracy was purchased with the shortened lives of the enslaved.

For those bound in this system, the phrase found its cruelest expression. Work began before dawn, in the darkness when sight was useless, and did not cease until night swallowed the fields once more. Exhaustion became the baseline, and survival required bending to the rhythm of the lash. Families were torn apart at the auction block; children grew up knowing separation is a commonplace reality. Autonomy was stolen, and culture was targeted for erasure.

And yet resistance flickered. Africans from Sierra Leone and the Windward Coast, chosen precisely for their expertise in rice cultivation, used that very knowledge to negotiate fragments of autonomy in the task system, carving out slivers of time to tend gardens, fish, and sustain their families. Spirituals rose in the fields, coded with double meanings prayers for deliverance, yes, but also roadmaps for escape. The Gullah-Geechee culture1, born in the low country isolation, preserved African languages, foodways, and spiritual practices, ensuring that the oppressors' system of erasure became instead a crucible of cultural survival.

The Carolinas became a paradox: a place of profound suffering and remarkable preservation, where a system built to erase Black humanity instead forged enduring legacies. The rice swamps and coastal plantations were sites of relentless cruelty, yet isolation in the Lowcountry allowed African languages, knowledge, spiritual practices, and social structures to endure. Under constant pressure, enslaved Africans did more than survive they remembered, adapted, and rebuilt, transforming suffering into continuity and outlasting the architects of their bondage.

From these swamps and fields from this furnace of cruelty and creativity, the roots of diasporic resilience took hold. Rhythm, language, faith, and resistance emerged as living archives, carried beyond the Carolinas into the Caribbean and across the Black world.

1 The Gullah-Geechee culture is a unique African American heritage rooted in the coastal regions of South Carolina, Georgia, and northern Florida, characterized by its

The Gang System and Task System

Labor on Carolina plantations was not random, it was engineered. Two dominant systems, the gang system and the task system, defined enslaved life, each designed with ruthless precision to maximize profit while tightening the grip of control. These were not mere methods of work; they were mechanisms of domination, calibrated to extract both body and spirit.

Figure 1 Each slave heading with his or her pickaxe for the plantation, where they work virtually naked. Jules David [del.] ; Budzilowicz [sc.]. 1850.

The **gang system**[2], common in upland cotton and tobacco areas but also present on some rice plantations, was the very image of industrialized slavery. Groups of twenty to fifty enslaved people moved in unison under the unrelenting eye of an overseer or a "driver." At times, that driver was an enslaved man given a fragile, dangerous elevation of status forced into the role of enforcer, torn between his own bondage and the master's demands.

2 The gang system was a labor organization method used on Southern plantations, where enslaved people were grouped into teams, or "gangs," to perform specific tasks under strict supervision, maximizing efficiency and control.

Work began at first light, when "can't see" described the darkness of dawn, and continued until sight was swallowed again by dusk. Hours stretched 14–16 in summer, with breaks dictated not by mercy but by the crack of a whip. The slowest worker risked punishment for all, creating a system where exhaustion bred resentment, but rebellion was quelled by fear. It was slavery reimagined as an assembly line inhuman, relentless, grinding from "can't see to can't see."

The **task system**[3], more prevalent in the Lowcountry's rice and indigo plantations, appeared gentler but was no less coercive. Here, enslaved workers were assigned daily quotas: clear a quarter-acre of swamp, hoe a fixed number of rows, or harvest a set weight of rice. Once the quota was met, any remaining time could be used for personal pursuits, such as gardening, fishing, family activities, or trading goods. This system drew from West African models of communal labor, and in its crevices, enslaved Africans carved out cultural survival. Gullah-Geechee practices, from language to farming traditions, thrived in these slivers of autonomy. Families grew produce, they bartered in local markets, and sometimes earned small incomes, planting seeds of independence long before the era of emancipation.

But this was no gift. Quotas were grueling, often designed to push the limits of endurance, and they escalated as planters grew greedier. Failure brought lashes just as in the gang system. What planters valued was not humanity but efficiency: the task system allowed them to extract labor while masking oppression with the illusion of choice.

3 The task system assigned enslaved individuals specific daily tasks, allowing them to manage their time after completion.

Figure 2 Rice culture on the Ogeechee, near Savannah, Georgia, 1867

Rice and Indigo Plantations

The Carolinas' rise to economic power rested on two labor-intensive crops of **rice** and **indigo** that transformed the Lowcountry into one of the wealthiest slave societies in the Americas. These plantations were not simply farms; they were sprawling, engineered landscapes, where enslaved Africans' knowledge and unrelenting labor created fortunes for white elites while trapping Black bodies in cycles of disease, isolation, and ceaseless toil.

Figure 3 Rice cultivation, 1600s

Rice cultivation, introduced in the late 1600s, flourished in the tidal swamps of South Carolina and Georgia. It was no accident: planters specifically targeted enslaved Africans from the "Rice Coast" of West Africa Sierra Leone, Gambia, and Senegal who carried centuries of expertise in wetland agriculture. Their knowledge of irrigation, dike construction, and crop rotation became the foundation of the Carolinas' wealth. Under the **task system,** enslaved workers built elaborate canals, dikes, and floodgates, bending rivers to the planter's will and transforming marshland into fertile fields. The result was "Carolina Gold" rice, a globally prized export that made Charleston the wealthiest city in British North America by the 18th century.

But this wealth came at a staggering cost. Rice cultivation demanded labor in knee-deep, mosquito-infested water, where malaria, dysentery, and yellow fever killed thousands. Work followed the seasons: planting seeds in spring mud, endless weeding in summer heat, harvesting in flooded autumn fields. Women bore burdens sowing seed, processing grain, pounding and winnowing by hand, yet their contributions were systematically erased from planter records. By 1800, more than 100,000 Africans had been trafficked through Charleston alone, embedding West African cultural memory in the Carolinas, where Gullah-Geechee traditions of language, food, and spirituality endure as living testaments of survival.

Indigo, the second crop, stained both fabric and flesh. Demand for the deep blue dye surged in the 1700s, transforming swaths of the Lowcountry into indigo estates processing required fermenting the plant in vats, releasing toxic fumes that scar lungs and burned skin. Enslaved people, especially women and children, worked long hours stirring, straining, and pressing the indigo cakes that enriched Europe's textile industries. The dye's vibrant blue fueled Charleston's rise as a global port, even as it poisoned those whose hands created it.

Together, rice and indigo made South Carolina a slave-powered powerhouse, rivaling the wealth of entire nations. They entrenched slavery more deeply than cotton ever could at the time, proving that the Carolinas were not simply agricultural regions but **laboratories,** where Black expertise was stolen and weaponized to build white fortunes. Yet, in the swamps and vats, amid death and degradation, enslaved Africans carved out culture, preserved memory, and planted seeds of endurance. The same fields that claimed lives also gave birth to resilience, shaping legacies that still resonate in the Carolinas and across the diaspora.

THE DEEP BLUE CROP OF THE LOWCOUNTRY

Figure 4 Workers harvest the indigo plant during the hot summer months. Engraving from a French book, circa 1760. Courtesy of the South Carolinia Library

The Deep Blue Crop of the Lowcountry

Figure 5 Portrait of Eliza Lucas Pinckney, credited with introducing and developing indigo as a major cash crop in colonial South Carolina during the 18th century.

Indigo, the "deep blue" dye crop, stood alongside rice as one of the Lowcountry's most profitable exports, its peak tied to Eliza Lucas Pinckney's innovations in the 1740s. But indigo was more than a crop, it was a system of exploitation. Enslaved Africans planted seeds in sandy soils, weeded fields under burning sun, and harvested leaves during sweltering summers. Processing was even more brutal: fermenting and agitating pulp in wooden vats produced choking fumes and toxic residues that scar lungs, burned skin, and sickened workers.

Planters relied on skilled enslaved "indigo makers" to oversee vats artisans whose knowledge and precision determined quality. Yet their expertise was stolen, their identities erased, their labor reduced to profit bricks of dye bound for British textile mills. An acre might yield 80 pounds of indigo, but at the cost of untold human suffering. By the time of the American Revolution, global competition had caused the decline of indigo. Still, its legacy remained: the Carolinas had been cemented as a slave society, where Black majorities in coastal districts terrified elites who remembered uprisings like the Stono Rebellion of 1739. Indigo's stain was permanent not just on cloth, but on bodies, laws, and culture.

Brutality, Family Separation, and Dehumanization

Beneath the fade of wealth, the Carolinas were laboratories of terror. The pillars of the plantation regime, **brutality, family separation, and dehumanization**, were not incidental but deliberate strategies of control, designed to crush resistance and turn human beings into tools.

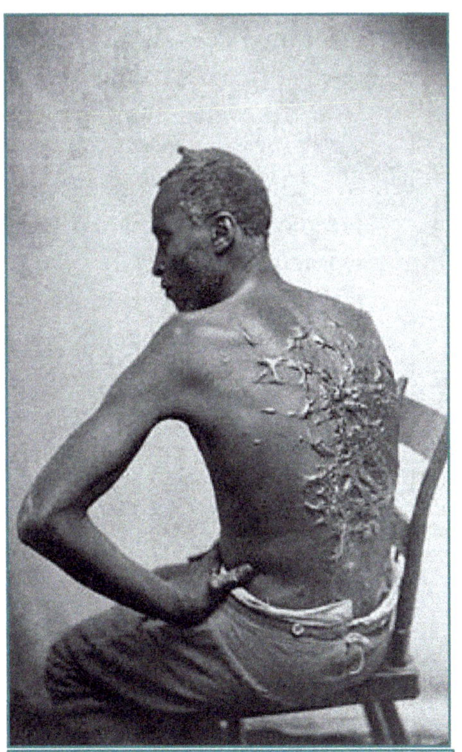

Figure 6 Scars of Peter, a whipped Louisiana slave, photographed in April 1863 and later distributed by abolitionists

Brutality was ever-present. Overseers wielded whips, stocks, and branding irons. Whippings of 100 lashes or more left backs carved like maps of pain, scars that bore witness long after emancipation. Laws allowed unlimited punishment so long as it did not technically result in death. Psychological violence accompanied the physical threats, humiliation, and forced witnessing of others' torment. Charles Ball, a formerly enslaved man, recalled collapsing workers dragged back to the rows, their bodies flogged until flesh split, then forced to keep working.

Family separation was equally devastating. Charleston's slave market, the largest in North America, auctioned husbands away from wives, mothers from children, siblings into different states. A nursing infant could be ripped from a mother's arms for sale, severing bonds essential to survival. These practices mirrored those in Caribbean colonies, where families were fractured to prevent collective resistance. The trauma stretched across generations, embedding loss into the cultural memory of the diaspora.

Figure 7 Whipping a Slave, Surinam, 1770s", Public Domain. Source: Slaveryimages.org

Dehumanization undergirded the system. Enslaved Africans were stripped of identity and reduced to property in ledgers. Laws forbade literacy, cultural expression, or self-defense. African names were erased, drums were banned, and women were subjected to systemic sexual violence that treated their bodies as breeding stock. Enslaved men, women, and children were inventoried alongside cattle, their humanity deliberately denied.

Yet, resistance endured. Songs cloaked in coded meaning, secret ring shouts, poisonings of livestock, and escapes to maroon communities testified that even in the shadow of terror, enslaved people refused to surrender spirit.

The Lasting Shadows

This triad brutality, separation, and dehumanization did not dissolve with emancipation. It simply changed form. What ended in law continued in practice, re-emerging through systems carefully designed to preserve the same outcomes while discarding the language of slavery. Sharecropping replaced chains with contracts, binding Black families to land they did not own and debts they could never fully repay. Convict leasing resurrected forced labor through the criminal justice system, where Black men were arrested for minor or fabricated offenses and leased to private companies to work mines, railroads, and farms under conditions often more lethal than slavery itself. Jim Crow laws codified exclusion, ensuring that freedom existed only in theory, while daily life remained governed by terror, surveillance, and enforced inferiority.

These systems were not failures of emancipation they were its management. They ensured that labor remained cheap, disposable, and controlled, while wealth continued to accumulate elsewhere. Families were fractured not only by auction blocks but by chain gangs, prison sentences, and forced migration. The plantation no longer needed a whip when the law itself performed the same function. In this way, the Carolinas did not abandon slavery; they refined it, embedding its logic into courts, labor markets, and social hierarchies that still shape life today.

The shadows stretch into the modern era with unsettling clarity. Wage theft, employment discrimination, and the concentration of Black labor in low-paying, high-risk industries echo the same extractive patterns of the past. Policing and incarceration continue to remove parents from homes and children from stability, perpetuating cycles of absence that mirror the family separations of earlier centuries. Neighborhoods once built by Black labor are stripped of resources, while residents are blamed for the poverty imposed upon them. The language has shifted, but the outcome remains consistent: labor without security, work without ownership, effort without inheritance.

Generational poverty is not accidental, it is structural. It is the cumulative result of being denied land after emancipation, excluded from credit and homeownership, barred from education and capital, and subjected to constant economic precarity. The same rice and indigo fortunes that built Charleston's grand homes were never redistributed; they were protected, multiplied, and passed down. Meanwhile, the descendants of those who created that wealth were left with exhaustion as their inheritance. When people are forced to labor endlessly just to survive, legacy becomes impossible. Survival consumes all available energy.

This is why this phrase endures. It names not only historical labor conditions but a continuing reality where work expands while opportunity contracts. It describes lives governed by urgency rather than choice, where rest feels dangerous and stillness feels like failure. It captures a psychological inheritance as much as an economic one learned belief that worth is measured by endurance, that struggle is normal, and that exhaustion is virtue. These beliefs did not arise organically; they were cultivated by systems that required constant output but offered no path to security.

To understand why we still labor we must confront these roots honestly and without nostalgia. This requires naming how rice, indigo, and human exploitation forged the Carolinas' wealth, and how that wealth shaped the nation's economic foundations. It requires acknowledging that the benefits of that system did not disappear with time; they were consolidated. And it requires rejecting the myth that progress alone heals wounds left unaddressed.

Only through this reckoning can repair begin. Ownership cannot emerge without truth. Healing cannot take place without accountability. The work ahead is not merely about remembering the past, but about dismantling the structures that carried it forward. Until labor leads to dignity, stability, and inheritance until it builds rather than drains those shadows will remain. And the routine from "can't see to can't see" will continue to define lives that deserve far more than survival.

Chapter 3

CARIBBEAN CHAINS

Across the turquoise waters from the Carolinas lay the Caribbean islands glittering jewels of empire that mask some of the harshest labor regimes in the Atlantic world. Jamaica, Barbados, the Bahamas, and Saint-Domingue (now Haiti) were not just colonies; they were engines of European wealth, built on the backs of Africans who were forced into slavery and worked to exhaustion in the production of sugar, indigo, and cotton. If the Carolinas were fields of endurance, the Caribbean was a death ground.

Figure 8 Enslaved Africans cutting sugarcane in Antigua, 1823. From Ten Views in the Island of Antigua by William Clark

On these islands, it was more than a phrase it was the measure of a life's exhaustion. One observer wrote of enslaved Africans trudging "from can't-see to can't-see, in blazing sun or cold rain, crossing unbridged rivers, occasionally dropping dead in their tracks." Later abolitionists would echo the truth plainly: ***"Black field hands were worked to death in a system from can't see to can't see."***

The Sugar Death Trap

Figure 9 10 Toussaint Louverture, leader of the Haitian Revolution, who rose from slavery to defeat the armies of France, Spain, and Britain, securing Haiti's independence in 1804.

Sugar was the Caribbean's gold, but for the enslaved it was poison. From cutting cane under the tropical sun to hauling stalks to the mills and tending boiling vats of syrup, every step consumed

bodies at a terrifying rate. Mortality was so high that the enslaved population could not sustain itself planters relied on a constant influx of Africans to replace the dead. Saint-Domingue alone imported nearly **800,000 Africans in the 18th century,** yet fewer than half survived to see emancipation. Unlike the Carolinas, where enslaved populations reproduced and planters "bred" new generations, the Caribbean devoured its workers faster than they could be born.

Empire's Crown Jewels

Jamaica became the crown jewel of Britain's empire, with vast plantations funneling profits back to London's banks. Barbados nicknamed "Little England," perfected the sugar model so efficiently that it was exported across the region. Haiti then Saint-Domingue, was the richest colony in the world by the late 1700s, producing nearly half the globe's sugar. Yet its wealth was built on unimaginable brutality, until the enslaved population rose in the **Haitian Revolution (1791–1804),** defeating the armies of France, Spain, and Britain to create the first Black republic in the modern world.

Resistance Without End

Despite terror, resistance never ceased.

- **Maroons** in Jamaica carved out free territories in the Blue Mountains, waging guerrilla wars that forced Britain to sign treaties.
- **Bussa's Rebellion** in Barbados (1816) mobilized thousands, so threatening that martial law was declared across the island.
- In the Bahamas, enslaved Africans resisted in quieter ways slowing work, sabotaging equipment, or fleeing by boat to Florida or Cuba.
- And Haiti's revolution showed the ultimate possibility: not just resistance, but victory.

Figure 12 Jamaican Maroons ambushing colonial forces in the mountains—a glimpse into guerrilla resistance tactics."

Every rebellion, every escape, every whispered plot proved the same truth: the enslaved were never passive, they were always reaching for freedom.

Despite terror, resistance never ceased. Maroons in Jamaica forced Britain into treaties through guerrilla warfare; Bussa's Rebellion in Barbados mobilized thousands and triggered island-wide martial law; in the Bahamas, enslaved Africans resisted through sabotage, slowed labor, and escape by sea; and in Haiti, resistance achieved its highest form victory. Together, these acts affirm one truth: the enslaved were never passive but always reaching for freedom.

Culture as Survival, Culture as Weapon

Amidst the brutality, Africans in the Caribbean preserved and adapted their cultures as acts of survival and defiance.

- In Jamaica, drumming, spiritual practices, and Creole languages bound people together, even when planters tried to ban them.
- In Haiti, Vodou rituals became organizing spaces for revolution, turning faith into a weapon of war.
- In Barbados, work songs carried coded messages of pain and resistance, transforming labor into testimony.

These traditions were also connected to the Carolinas, where the Gullah-Geechee culture retained African words, rhythms, and farming practices proof that even across the oceans, the diaspora carried memory as a shield.

A Shared Struggle

The same ships that carried Africans to Charleston's rice swamps also brought them to Jamaica's cane fields and Haiti's boiling houses. The same chains shackled them, the same whips scarred their backs, the same exhaustion bent their bodies. Yet they shared more than suffering they shared survival, culture, and the will to resist.

The story of the Caribbean is not only one of brutality, but also one of endurance and rebellion. If sugar was the empire's lifeblood, then the enslaved were its heartbeat, and that heartbeat never stopped fighting for freedom. From the Carolinas to the Caribbean, the cry was the same: ***we will not labor from can't see to can't forever.***

Amidst the brutality, enslaved Africans refused to be reduced to machines of labor. Their resistance was not only in open rebellion but in the quiet, daily acts of survival and defiance. On Sundays, when some planters allowed a sliver of reprieve, enslaved people planted provision grounds, grew food for trade, and even carved out underground economies that sustained families against the system's intent. Music, dance, and spirituality became powerful tools of resilience: the drums that planters tried to silence in Jamaica continued to beat in maroon camps; Vodou ceremonies in Saint-Domingue sparked revolutionary resolve; and work songs in Barbados encoded messages of endurance and defiance.

These cultural strongholds were more than outlets of expression; they were declarations of humanity in a world that sought to erase it. Faith systems, oral traditions, and communal ties stitched together new identities across the diaspora, proving that even when bodies were broken, spirits endured.

The Caribbean's story is not only one of sugar's cruelty but of fire forged in struggle. Where labor was meant to kill, it birthed revolt. Where families were torn apart, they built kinship networks of survival. Where the empire sought to silence them, they created languages, songs, and faiths that still echo today.

The same ships that carried Africans to Charleston's rice fields brought them to Jamaica's cane brakes and Haiti's boiling houses. Across waters, the cries were the same: ***we will not labor from can't see to can't see forever.*** And in Haiti's revolution, in Jamaica's Maroon wars, in Barbados' rebellions, and in the quiet resistance of Bahamian shores, that cry was answered with a truth empire could not contain, ***freedom is inevitable when a people refuse to die in chains.***

Figure 13 Bussa, an enslaved African in Barbados, led a massive revolt in April 1816. Though suppressed, it became a defining moment in the island's struggle for freedom. Emancipation Statue, Barbados.

Amidst the brutality, enslaved Africans refused to let their voices be silenced. They carved out humanity where the system demanded dehumanization. A work song from Barbados, recorded in the late 18th century, begins:

Massa buy me, he won't killa me … For I live with an evil man.

Its lines capture the cruel absurdity of being reduced to property, yet they also reveal hidden resilience, the insistence on singing, on naming pain, on turning suffering into rhythm. These were not just laments; they were living archives, preserving memory, hope, and defiance across generations.

The story of these islands is not solely one of chains and whips it is equally one of resistance, survival, and connection. The same ships that carried Africans to Charleston's rice fields carried others to Jamaica's cane brakes, to Barbados' boiling houses, to Haiti's revolutionary streets. The same scars marked their backs. The same songs lifted their spirits. The same dreams of freedom stirred in their souls.

Together, these shared histories remind us that while the diaspora's chains were forged into different colonies, they were broken by the same unyielding will to be free. Across waters, across empires, across centuries, the cry was the same: we are more than labor, more than property, more than shadows in the fields.

Figure 14 Despite the brutality of slavery, African traditions survived in music, craftsmanship, and community, weaving resilience into Caribbean identity

Despite the brutality of slavery, African traditions refused to die. They lived on in music, craftsmanship, spirituality, and community woven into the very fabric of Caribbean identity. Drums, once outlawed, beat in hidden clearings. Folktales carried wisdom across generations. Skills in farming, building, and healing sustained communities even when systems sought to erase them. What survived was not just culture, it was a blueprint for resilience.

And when freedom finally came, the voices of its architects rang like thunder across the Atlantic. Haitian leader Toussaint Louverture declared:

"I was born a slave, but nature gave me the soul of a free man."

From the hills of Jamaica, Maroon chieftain Queen Nanny immortalized in legend and honored as a national hero warned her people to defend liberty at any cost:

"Death before slavery."

These words, born in struggle, still echo across the Caribbean, reminding us that even in the darkest cane fields and boiling houses, the flame of freedom was never extinguished. Instead, it was passed like a torch from rebellion to rebellion, from ancestor to descendant until it ignited revolutions that reshaped the world.

Slavery under British Rule in the Bahamas, French Rule in Haiti, and Across the Caribbean

The enslavement systems of the Caribbean mirroring and expanding on those in the Carolinas were laboratories of exploitation. In every colony, European powers perfected methods to extract the maximum profit from African labor, transforming tropical landscapes into engines of wealth for empires. What bound these systems together was not just the crops sugar, cotton, coffee, indigo but the relentless demand that enslaved Africans work "from can't see to can't see," until bodies broke and generations were consumed.

The Bahamas, under British rule, operated differently from Jamaica and Barbados, but shared the same core cruelty. Its shallow soils and scattered islands were less suited for vast sugar estates, so Bahamian slavery turned to cotton, salt raking, and maritime labor. Enslaved Bahamians endured blistering heat in salt ponds, hauling heavy loads across sharp crystals that cut their feet raw. Others were forced into fishing and ship work, extending bondage onto the sea itself. Isolation on small islands deepened control escape was rare, and the constant selling and shipping of people across the archipelago fragmented families.

Haiti, under French rule, was the opposite extreme: the wealthiest colony in the world by the late 1700s, its sugar and coffee plantations fueling France's global empire. But that wealth came at a staggering cost. Mortality rates were so high that enslaved Africans were literally worked to death, replaced by new captives from the Middle Passage in a cycle of relentless consumption. It was slavery at its most lethal, producing riches for Paris while burying Africans in unmarked graves. Yet Haiti also became the site of slavery's most dramatic reversal: the Haitian Revolution, led by Toussaint Louverture, Dessalines, and others, turned the world's most prosperous slave colony into the first Black republic in 1804 a beacon of resistance feared by every colonial power.

Across **Jamaica, Barbados, and the wider Caribbean,** British planters forged plantation societies where sugar was king and human lives expendable. Jamaica became Britain's "crown jewel," its profits underwriting the empire's industrial rise. Barbados nicknamed "Little England," pioneered the plantation model exported across the Caribbean, embedding a culture of extraction and racial hierarchy. Enslaved Africans worked under a regime of terror,lash, chain, and branding yet found ways to preserve African traditions through music, religion, and maroon resistance.

Despite the variations in geography and crops, the throughline was the same: European greed demanded African blood. Whether in the salt flats of Inagua, the coffee hills of Saint-Domingue, or the cane fields of Barbados, labor was endless, suffering was systemic, and survival itself was a form of resistance. The Caribbean was not a collection of islands but a connected web of oppression and, ultimately, a connected web of defiance. The same ships, laws, and plantation logics moved across these waters, binding distant shores into a single economy of exploitation. Yet resistance traveled those routes as well, carried through revolt, marronage, culture, and memory, proving that wherever bondage spread, so too did the will to break it.

British Rule in the Bahamas

Figure 15 Loyalist refugees arrive in the Bahamas during the late 18th century, bringing enslaved Africans from the American South to establish plantations and rebuild their lives under British rule.

In the Bahamas, British slavery evolved from the chaotic days of piracy and settlement in the 1600s into a more structured plantation system by the 18th century. The scattered islands stretching from Eleuthera to Grand Bahama and beyond saw their enslaved populations swell dramatically after the 1780s, when Loyalists fleeing the American Revolution brought thousands of enslaved Africans with them from the Carolinas and Georgia. These Loyalists, many of whom had grown rich from rice, indigo, and cotton in the American South, sought to recreate their fortunes in Bahamian soil. Alongside them came enslaved Africans transported directly through the same Middle Passage that fed Carolina's plantations, binding the Bahamas to the broader Atlantic system of bondage.

While the Bahamas lacked the sprawling rice plantations of South Carolina or the vast sugar estates of Jamaica, its labor demands were no less brutal. Enslaved people were forced into cotton cultivation of sea island, salt raking in blinding sun and razor-sharp flats, sponge diving in treacherous waters, and wreck salvaging from dangerous reefs. Each task carried its own risks: salt work stripped skin raw and left lasting wounds; diving and salvaging exposed enslaved Africans to drowning or shark attacks. Unlike plantation economies confined to fields, Bahamian slavery expanded onto the sea itself, extracting labor from both land and ocean.

British slave codes in the Bahamas mirrored the harshness of Carolina's Negro Acts, stripping Africans of legal protections and criminalizing even the smallest acts of autonomy whether learning to read, gathering without permission, or attempting to cultivate independent livelihoods. Families were torn apart in sales across islands; rebellions were swiftly crushed with violence. Yet, even in this system of calculated dehumanization, African resilience endured. Bahamian enslaved communities carried with them fragments of language, music, and spiritual traditions that would later shape Junkanoo, bush medicine, and Afro-Bahamian identity.

The Bahamas thus became a mirror of the Carolinas and the wider British Caribbean an archipelago where the empire's greed demanded backbreaking labor. Its waters sparkled to outsiders, but its shores were lined with the sweat, suffering, and survival of generations bound in chains.

What set the Bahamian system apart was how exploitation was scattered and normalized across islands and trades, making it harder to resist and easier to hide. Enslaved people were constantly moved between cays, tasks, and owners denied the stability needed to build power or security. This fragmentation outlived slavery itself. Emancipation arrived without land, repair, or economic footing, leaving generations navigating systems where survival required constant motion rather than rooted freedom. "Can't see to can't see" thus endured not just as a measure of labor, but as a lasting condition shaped by instability and unfinished justice.

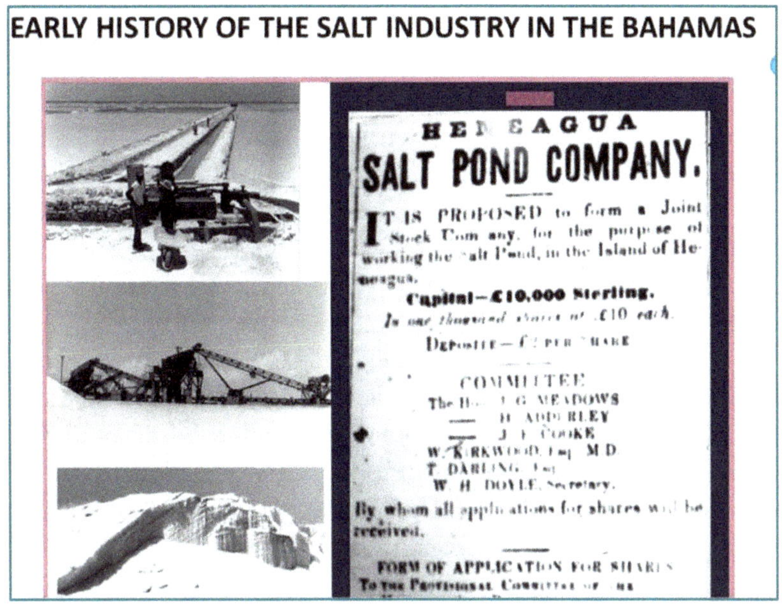
EARLY HISTORY OF THE SALT INDUSTRY IN THE BAHAMAS

HE[illegible]EAGUA

SALT POND COMPANY.

IT IS PROPOSED to form a Joint Stock Company, for the purpose of working the Salt Pond, in the Island of Heneagua.

Capital—£10,000 Sterling.

In one thousand shares of £10 each.

Deposit—£[illegible] per Share

COMMITTEE

The Hon. [illegible] G. MEADOWS
— [illegible] ADDERLEY
— J. F. COOKE
W. KIRKWOOD, Esq. M.D.
T. DARLING, Esq.
W. H. DOYLE, Secretary.

By whom all applications for shares will be received.

FORM OF APPLICATION FOR SHARES

To the Provisional Committee of [illegible]

Figure 4 Workers harvest the indigo plant during the hot summer months. Engraving from a French book, circa 1760. Courtesy of the South Caroliniana Library

Resistance in the Bahamas

Resistance persisted, even on islands where planters and colonial officials assumed that isolation characterized by scattered settlements and remote cays would prevent rebellion. Yet Maroons slipped into hidden cays and mangroves, building free enclaves and surviving through fishing, farming, and secret trade with sympathetic sailors. Organized uprisings also erupted: the **1831 Golden Grove revolution**[4] Jamaica, where enslaved Africans openly defied their masters, echoed the larger rebellions that shook Barbados and Demerara[5] in the same era.

4 1831 Golden Grove revolt – A local outbreak of Jamaica's wider Baptist War, where Demerara was a former British colony on the northern coast of South America, in whit is today Guyana.

After Britain outlawed the transatlantic slave trade in 1807, the Bahamas became a destination for "recaptives" Africans rescued from illegal slave ships by the Royal Navy and resettled in the colony. Though legally free, many were subjected to mandatory "apprenticeship" periods, a system that restricted their freedom and mirrored slavery. By 1834, when emancipation was enacted, approximately 10,000 enslaved individuals made up most of the the Bahamas' population. Yet, they were largely denied access to land, wealth, and the resources their labor had produced.

Even surnames tell the story of bondage and survival. Today, Bahamian names like **Johnson, Rolle, Curry, Pinder, Fernander, Minns, and Sweeting** trace back not to African lineages but to Loyalist slaveholders, overseers, or the colonial system that imposed them. Recaptives often inherited these imposed identities as well, erasing their original African names and replacing them with European markers of ownership and control. Each Bahamian surname, then, carries the weight of a dual inheritance: a reminder of both forced assimilation and the endurance of African-descended peoples who forged culture, kinship, and survival despite displacement.

French Rule in Haiti (Saint-Domingue)

Meanwhile, in **Saint-Domingue,** France's Caribbean crown jewel, slavery reached an intensity unparalleled in the hemisphere. By the late 1700s, the colony produced nearly half the world's sugar and coffee, feeding Europe's insatiable appetite. This wealth came at an extraordinary human cost: more than **773,000 Africans** were imported, a population outnumbering whites by nearly ten to one, and governed under the draconian **Code Noir**[6]**,** which prescribed brutal punishments, restricted freedoms, and enforced Catholic conversion.

6 The Code Noir (1685) was a French law governing slavery in colonies, defining enslaved Africans as property, mandating Catholic baptism, enforcing harsh punishments, and limiting free people of color's rights. It did not apply to the British-controlled Bahamas.

Labor was relentless, organized under the **gang system,** where enslaved people toiled from "can't see to can't see" in sweltering cane fields and boiling houses, their lives often cut short within a decade of arrival. Mortality rates were so severe that planters depended on a constant influx of new Africans, treating them as disposable. Yet even in this crucible of suffering, **marronage thrived.** Enslaved Africans fled to the mountains, forming maroon communities that waged guerrilla warfare and struck alliances with the **gens de couleur** the free people of color, many of whom owned property and sometimes enslaved people themselves, yet were barred from full equality under French rule. These tensions created a volatile society where every layer of oppression and resistance interlocked, setting the stage for the world-shaking **Haitian Revolution** of 1791.

The Haitian Revolution and Its Reverberations

The **1791 Bois Caïman ceremony**[7] marked more than a spiritual gathering it was the spark that lit the fuse of the most consequential uprising in the Atlantic world. Enslaved Africans, bound by chains yet united by faith, drums, and oath, launched a revolt that would evolve into the **Haitian Revolution.** Under the leadership of **Toussaint Louverture, Jean-Jacques Dessalines**, and Henri Christophe, they defeated the armies of France, Spain, and Britain three of the greatest empires of the age. By 1804, Haiti declared independence, birthing the **first Black republic** and forever shattering the myth of Black inferiority upon which slavery rested.

7 large-scale slave uprising against French colonial rule in Saint-Domingue (modern-day Haiti).The Bois Caïman Ceremony of August 1791 was a pivotal event in the Haitian Revolution, marking the start of the

This seismic event sent **shockwaves through the Carolinas and across the Atlantic world.** Planters in Charleston whispered in terror that their own enslaved populations might rise; new restrictions and slave codes were tightened to prevent "contagion." Across the Caribbean, enslaved people drew inspiration from singing about Haiti as a beacon of hope. The revolution proved that the laboring masses once thought broken from "can't see to can't see" could seize destiny and create freedom.

Jamaica and Barbados

Other Caribbean colonies bore the same scars and seeds of defiance. In **Jamaica,** Maroon communities carved free towns deep in the **Blue Mountains,** sustaining themselves through guerrilla warfare and raids on plantations. Despite treaties with the British, their very existence challenged colonial authority, showing that fugitives could outlast an empire. Resistance never ceased: Tacky's Revolt of 1760[8] and later uprisings inspired future generations who would eventually push toward emancipation.

In **Barbados,** branded "Little England" for its rigid plantation hierarchy, sugar profits propped up Britain's wealth, but the system was brittle. In **1816, Bussa's Rebellion**[9] Led by an African-born enslaved man, they mobilized thousands in a daring insurrection. Though crushed, it exposed cracks in the colonial order and symbolized a growing refusal to accept the endless grind. Barbados' fields, like Jamaica's cane rows and Haiti's boiling houses, became stages of both unbearable exploitation and audacious resistance.

8 Tacky's Revolt (1760) was a major Jamaican slave uprising led by Akan leader Tacky against British plantations. Crushed by colonial forces, it led to executions and deportations.

9 Bussa's Rebellion (1816), Barbados' largest slave uprising, led by Igbo-born Bussa, began April 14 at Bayley's Plantation. Involving 20,000 enslaved people, it was crushed by British forces, with Bussa and hundreds killed or executed.

Sugarcane Labor as a High-Mortality Industry

No crop embodied the Caribbean's deadly alchemy like **sugarcane** a so-called "white gold" that devoured human lives faster than it enriched empires. Across the vast estates of **Haiti, Jamaica, and Barbados,** as well as the smaller but equally brutal fields of **Trinidad, Grenada, Antigua, and the Bahamas** (where sugar supplemented cotton), cane plantations operated as factories in the open air. Under the crack of the whip, enslaved Africans endured relentless gang labor from ***"can't see to can't see,"*** swinging machetes at dawn and collapsing only after nightfall. The cycle did not end in the field's cut stalks were hauled into **boiling houses,** where scalding vats of syrup filled the air with toxic fumes that seared lungs and blistered skin. Mortality rates soared so high that enslaved populations rarely reproduced themselves; deaths outpaced births, forcing planters to replenish their labor force by dragging in new captives from West Africa. In the ruthless calculus of empire, Black bodies were **expendable fuel burned up to keep the machinery of colonial wealth alive.**

The labor cycle was nothing short of a **gauntlet of death.** It began with land clearance: enslaved workers hacked through jungles, felled hardwood trees, dug drainage canals, and planted cane shots under a blazing sun, often waist-deep in mud swarming with leeches and parasites. The harvest season was the most punishing stretch of all. From first light to darkness, gangs of men and women swung machetes at stalks as tall as a man, their razor-sharp leaves slicing open bare arms and faces until skin hung in ribbons. Cane juice attracted swarms of insects, while every cut risked festering into a deadly infection in the tropical humidity. Behind them, children and elders dragged the heavy bundles to carts, feeding mills that crushed stalks into pulp. Inside the boiling houses, enslaved "sugar boilers" often highly skilled and highly endangered labored in suffocating heat, stirring scalding syrup while enduring the constant threat of burns, explosions, and collapse from exhaustion.

So lethal was the industry that in places like **Jamaica,** the average lifespan of an enslaved African after arrival was just **seven years.** In Barbados, planters calculated that it was cheaper to ***"work a slave to death and buy another"*** than to allow rest or care. Even the Bahamas, with smaller-scale sugar operations, mirrored this brutality, pairing it with salt-raking and cotton cultivation. Everywhere, sugar's profits poured into the coffers of London, Paris, and Amsterdam, while African lives were ground into ash.

Sugarcane, more than any other crop, explains why ***"from can't see to can't see"*** was not just a phrase but a death sentences a life measured in sweat, blood, and the few short years before the grave. Yet, within this furnace of oppression, songs, resistance, and the whisper of freedom still endured, proving that even the most dehumanizing labor could not fully extinguish the human will to be free.

Infernos of the Boiling Houses

If the cane fields were brutal, the **boiling houses** were hell itself factories of fire where enslaved Africans worked in conditions so deadly that survival was often measured in seasons, not years. Within stone-walled chambers, stalks were fed into iron rollers machines so unforgiving that one slip could shear off a hand or crush an arm in an instant. The cane juice, gushing like blood from the rollers, was hauled into great copper vats, where enslaved "sugar boilers" stirred scalding syrup in a haze of steam and suffocating fumes. The air itself became a weapon: hot, damp, and thick with smoke that scorched lungs, blurred vision, and choked the breath from weary bodies. Crop season blurred into a nightmare of **16 to 18-hour days,** with exhaustion broken only by the crack of the overseer's whip.

Mortality was not incidental; it was **built into the system.** In Haiti the empire of sugar the annual death rate hovered between **5–10%,** meaning entire enslaved populations had to be replaced every decade. Life expectancy for a newly arrived field slave could be as little as **five years.** In Jamaica, British records acknowledged grimly that "the Negroes die faster than they can be born," necessitating the constant importation of new captives from Africa. Barbados, dubbed **"Little England,"** was even more merciless: its dense plantations left no land for enslaved people to cultivate food, and starvation stalked the cane rows. In Trinidad, Antigua, and Grenada, both French and British planters drove their enslaved populations through wet and dry seasons without respite, grinding bodies into the ground before a decade had passed.

Disease added another blade to the whip. Malaria thrived in mosquito-choked canals; yellow fever swept through settlements with every rain; dysentery festered in the worm-ridden cornmeal and rancid salt fish passed off as rations. Women worked until childbirth and were forced back into the fields soon after, their bodies broken by labor. Children, too young to stand steady, were sent to weed and haul, their spines bending under loads meant for grown men. Infant mortality soared beyond **50%** on some islands, a generational culling that ensured plantations would forever hunger for fresh African lives.

Across the Caribbean, from the northern plains of Haiti to Jamaica's cane brakes and Barbados's wind-swept estates, sugar was not agriculture it was a **machine of death,** a slow-motion execution whose victims powered the fortunes of Europe. This was the empire's cruelest arithmetic: lives measured not in years or legacies, but in the pounds of sugar shipped abroad. And yet even here, amid the flames of the boiling house songs were sung, prayers whispered, and rebellions plotted, proof that while the system consumed Black bodies, it could never fully extinguish their spirit.

Figure 18 Enslaved Africans forced to bend over sugarcane in 18th-century Caribbean fields—a visual reminder of cane cultivation's brutal cycle of unrelenting labor and vulnerability to injury and disease.

Sugar in the Bahamas: A Secondary but Deadly Crop

In the Bahamas, sugar never reached the scale of Jamaica or Barbados, yet it carved scars just as deep. On Loyalist estates in Andros and Cat Island, the methods mirrored the Jamaican model gang labor from "can't see to can't see," overseers' whips cutting through the humid air, and lives consumed by cane. Here, however, coral-studded soils added an extra cruelty: enslaved Africans hacked through limestone with primitive tools, dug trenches by hand, and hauled seawater-irrigated soil under a sun so fierce it blistered the skin. Sugar was not just backbreaking it was bone breaking. Even in smaller outputs, the crop demanded everything and returned only death.

Across the Caribbean, sugar was less an industry than a **death trade.** More than **five million Africans** were dragged into the region over three centuries because natural reproduction was impossible under such conditions. Annual death rates between **3–7%** made the system self-consuming, requiring constant replenishment from the Middle Passage. The enslaved were not valued as people, or even as long-term workers, but as **disposable fuel** to be burned up in the furnaces of empire.

Brutality magnified the toll. Whippings for "slow" work sliced flesh to the bone, and wounds were rubbed with salt, pepper, or lime to intensify the agony. Some were "broken" deliberately: hoisted by their limbs, branded, mutilated, or locked in wooden stocks for days under the open sky. Yet, the system never crushed the spirit of resistance. Enslaved workers jammed iron into rollers to sabotage mills, set cane fields ablaze in the night, poisoned overseers, and escaped into the wild,joining maroon communities on uninhabited cays. These acts of defiance echoed the larger revolts of the Americas, from the Stono Rebellion of **1739**[10] in South Carolina to the **Haitian Revolution** itself, proving that even under unthinkable oppression, the will to resist remained unbroken.

The sugar machine whether in Jamaica, Haiti, Barbados, or Antigua was built on high turnover and low regard for human life. Labor was cheap, replaceable, and expendable, treated no differently than the stalks discarded after the juice had been boiled out. This ruthless arithmetic enriched French and British elites, turning London, Paris, and Bristol into global centers of commerce, while the people whose bodies built that wealth were left in hunger and chains.

10 Stono Rebellion (1739) was a significant slave uprising in South Carolina, led by an enslaved man named Jemmy (or Cato), likely of Kongo origin. It was one of the largest and deadliest slave revolts in the British American colonies, challenging the plantation system.

Emancipation in 1834 promised freedom but delivered limited gains in the Bahamas and Haiti. Freed Africans, legally liberated, were denied land, capital, and opportunities. In the Bahamas, British slaveholders received **substantial compensation,** securing their wealth, while the formerly enslaved faced exploitative labor systems like sharecropping and low-wage work, perpetuating poverty. Haiti's post-revolutionary struggles, including French indemnity payments, similarly entrenched economic hardship. These systems, though not slavery in name, maintained economic oppression, binding generations to systemic inequality.

This is the shadow that lingers still: an inheritance of exploitation where the wealth of empire rests on the unmarked graves of those who labored from "can't see to can't see."

Emancipation and Apprenticeship in the Bahamas

In The Bahamas, British emancipation in **1834** came not as liberation but as an illusion chained to a four-year ***"apprenticeship"*** system that replicated slavery under another name. Men and women were still compelled to labor without wages for their former masters, up to **45 hours per week,** their "freedom" hemmed in by overseers, magistrates, and the whip. Children under six were nominally freed, but every other man, woman, and youth was bound until **1838;** their labor was now legitimized rather than humane.

The apprenticeship period was little more than a continuation of bondage. Punishments for "laziness" or "insolence" ranged from imprisonment to flogging, while colonial courts invariably sided with planters. Even after its formal end, freedom was crippled by deliberate economic sabotage. **Land, the true foundation of independence was withheld.** Colonial elites monopolized crown lands (and still due to this day), forcing the newly emancipated into exploitative arrangements, such as sharecropping, which depleted soils, working salt ponds under a burning sun, or diving for sponges in shark-infested waters. The infamous **"truck system[11]"** paid laborers not in money but in overpriced goods from company stores, trapping entire families in cycles of debt indistinguishable from slavery.

Adding insult to injury, emancipation came with **compensation for the enslavers, not the enslaved.** Britain funneled **£126,848, equivalent to over $20 million today,** into the pockets of **1,057 Bahamian slaveowners** for the "loss" of their 10,087 enslaved people. The emancipated themselves received nothing but poverty and the expectation of continuing to work the same fields for the same masters. As historian Eric Williams noted, emancipation was financed not for justice but for the protection of colonial capital.

By the 1840s, the impossibility of survival in the Bahamas without land or fair wages spurred **mass migration.** Bahamians sailed to Florida to cut timber and cultivate crops, to Cuba's sugar fields and coffee groves, and to the salt flats of Turks and Caicos in search of income. At home, export economies in cotton, **salt, and pineapples** only deepened dependency on white mercantile elites, who controlled trade and credit into the mid-20th century.

Freedom, then, was shadowed by betrayal. Emancipation promised dawn but delivered a dim twilight where Bahamians lived unchained in body but shackled by poverty, colonial law, and the memory of a debt Britain never repaid.

11 The truck system paid workers in goods or credit instead of cash, trapping freed people in the Bahamas in economic dependency post-1834. Prevalent in agriculture and sponging, it reinforced exploitative labor systems, akin to "class slavery."

Haiti, emerging from its revolutionary war of independence (1791–1804), faced a parallel yet distinct betrayal. Unlike the gradual **British model[12],** Haiti's enslaved population violently overthrew French rule, establishing the world's first Black republic in 1804 and permanently banning slavery the only successful slave revolt in history. Yet, freedom came at a staggering cost: France demanded reparations for the "loss" of slaves, property, and the colony itself, imposing an independence debt of 150 million francs (reduced to 90 million) in 1825 under threat of invasion and slavery's restoration.

This extortion, equivalent to $21 billion in modern terms, weakened Haiti's economy; payments, financed through foreign loans, continued until 1947, diverting resources from development and enforcing poverty. Land reform after the revolution saw plantations broken into smallholdings for former slaves, fostering a peasant-based agrarian society. However, the debt and international isolation U.S. recognition was delayed until 1862 due to fears of inspiring slave revolts prevented the country from achieving prosperity.

Haiti and the Bahamas reveal two paths out of slavery one through revolution, the other through reform but both were punished for Black freedom. In each case, emancipation was followed by economic containment, debt, and deliberate underdevelopment designed to protect imperial wealth. Communities survived by building parallel systems whether through Haiti's *lakou*[13] or Bahamian kinship networks, but survival was not the same as justice. The chains were removed, yet the cost of freedom was engineered to endure, ensuring that "can't see to can't see" lived on not as law, but as inherited reality.

12 The "gradual British model" refers to the British Empire's phased approach to abolishing slavery via the 1833 Slavery Abolition Act (effective 1834), which ended chattel slavery but imposed a 4–6 year "apprenticeship" period of unpaid labor for former slaves, while compensating owners with £20 million (equivalent to billions today), contrasting with immediate or revolutionary emancipations like Haiti's.

13 In Haitian culture, a "lakou" (from Kreyòl for "courtyard" or "yard") refers to a traditional rural compound or communal living space where extended families or neighbors share a central yard surrounded by multiple homes, serving as a social, economic, spiritual, and cultural hub often tied to Vodou practices and inherited land

Haiti's Revolutionary Triumph and Crushing Debt

Haiti's path to freedom was both triumphant and punishing. On **January 1, 1804,** after more than a decade of unrelenting struggle, the Haitian Revolution culminated in victory. Enslaved Africans and their descendants led by Toussaint Louverture, Jean-Jacques Dessalines, and Henri Christophe defeated the combined forces of **France, Spain, and Britain,** three of the world's greatest empires. Haiti emerged as the **world's first Black republic,** permanently abolishing slavery and proving that the enslaved could not only rise but rule. It was the only successful slave revolt in history that created a sovereign nation.

Yet the triumph of 1804 was quickly shackled by the machinery of global white supremacy. In **1825**, King Charles X of France dispatched **14 warships** to hover menacingly off the coast of Port-au-Prince, their cannons trained on the new republic. The message was unmistakable: accept France's terms or face re-invasion and re-enslavement. Haiti was forced to agree to an **"indemnity" of 150 million francs** (later reduced to 90 million) to compensate French planters for their "lost property," which included the very people who had liberated themselves.

This **ransom for freedom** was financed through crushing loans from French banks at high interest, binding Haiti to a century of debt. The burden did not end until **1947,** with payments totaling **112 million francs** but the actual cost was incalculable. Historians estimate that between **$21 billion and $115 billion in lost growth was siphoned away, money that could have been used to build roads, schools, ports, and hospitals.** Instead, it flowed back into European coffers, leaving Haiti impoverished. To put this in perspective, the indemnity equaled nearly **300% of Haiti's current GDP** a catastrophic handicap imposed on a newborn nation.

Thus, the revolution that inspired freedom movements from the Carolinas to South America was punished with economic strangulation. Haiti had broken slavery's chains with blood and fire, but France and its allies forged **new chains of debt and isolation** that ensured Black sovereignty would be impoverished.

Broken Promises and Generational Poverty

Figure 19 Jean-Jacques Dessalines (born c. 1758, West Africa—died October 17, 1806, Pont Rouge, near Port-au-Prince, Haiti) was the emperor of Haiti who proclaimed his country's independence in 1804.

When Haiti shattered the chains of slavery, its people expected freedom to mean land, security, and dignity. Yet the reality was far harsher. Former slaves received **no reparations** only the crushing indemnity to France and continued economic strangulation. Leaders like **Jean-Jacques Dessalines** attempted to transform the dream into reality in his 1805 land redistribution decree, which involved breaking up plantations and granting smallholdings to peasants, freedmen, and soldiers. For a brief moment, Haiti looked poised to redefine freedom as ownership.

But internal fractures undermined that vision. Class divisions hardened between the **Black majority peasantry** and the lighter-skinned **mulatto elite,** who often sought to preserve wealth and privilege at the expense of broader equality. Corruption and authoritarianism deepened the nation's cracks, while international isolation starved it of trade and allies. The United States, fearful of sparking uprisings among its enslaved population, refused to recognize Haitian independence until **1862**, nearly six decades after its founding.

For ordinary Haitians, land meant survival but not prosperity. The breakup of estates into fragmented small plots fostered **lakou**[14], communal agrarian compounds rooted in African tradition. While lakou provided solidarity and cultural resilience, it locked peasants into subsistence farming. Without access to credit, tools, or broader markets, they remained vulnerable to famine, hurricanes, earthquakes, and foreign meddling. When the United States invaded and occupied Haiti from 1915 to 1934, it further entrenched systems of exploitation, forcing peasants into road labor and deepening cycles of dependency.

This Haitian betrayal mirrors the story of the wider Black diaspora. In the U.S. South, freedmen were promised **"40 acres and a mule"** under General Sherman's Special Field Order No. 15[15] in 1865. That land redistribution could have laid the foundation for Black prosperity, but President Andrew Johnson rescinded it, returning confiscated estates to Confederate planters. The result was sharecropping and generational poverty, just as in Haiti, where land was too little and reparations were inverted paid not to the enslaved, but to their former masters.

The lesson is clear: **freedom without ownership is an illusion.** Whether in Haiti's hills, the Carolinas' cotton fields, or the Bahamas' salt ponds, emancipation often meant exchanging slavery for endless labor under new guises. Without land, capital, or reparations, the descendants of the enslaved inherited poverty instead of prosperity, their sweat still enriching others.

---

14 Lakou: Communal Haitian compounds formed post-1804 from fragmented estate plots, rooted in African traditions. These agrarian, family-based units with Vodou shrines ensured survival but not prosperity for ordinary Haitians

15 Special Field Order No. 15 (1865): Issued by Gen. Sherman, it allocated 400,000 acres in SC-GA-FL to freedmen in 40-acre plots. Revoked by Pres. Johnson, returning land to Confederates, it left freedmen in poverty, unlike Haiti's lakou system.

Barbados: "Little England" and the Long Shadow of Apprenticeship

Barbados, often hailed by the British as ***"Little England"*** for its loyal imitation of imperial society, became one of the clearest examples of emancipation betrayed. When slavery was abolished in 1834 under the British Slavery Abolition Act, freedom was shackled to a **four-year apprenticeship system,**a sleight of hand that extended bondage under another name. Former slaves were compelled to labor up to **45 hours per week without pay** for their former masters, their movements restricted by **vagrancy laws** that criminalized unemployment. Flogging and the treadmill were used to enforce discipline, ensuring that the old system of control endured beneath the thin veneer of reform.

Resistance, however, was fierce. Protests, work stoppages, and relentless defiance forced Britain to **end apprenticeship early in 1838,** a victory for the emancipated. Yet when freedom finally came, it was freedom without foundation. **Land the key to independence, remained in planter hands.** Former slaves received no reparations, no plots to build upon, no capital to launch new lives. Instead, they were pushed back onto sugar estates under **metayer contracts,** a sharecropping arrangement that bound them to the very plantations where they had once been enslaved, their wages consumed by rents and debts to the white planter class.

Meanwhile, Britain showered wealth on the enslavers. Across its empire, slaveowners received **£20 million in compensation** the equivalent of **£17 billion today** for the "loss" of their human property. In Barbados, planters claimed large shares for the **83,000 enslaved people** they had owned. The newly freed, by contrast, got nothing but poverty. It was the same script playing out across the diaspora: in the Bahamas under "apprenticeship," in Haiti under the French indemnity, and in the United States, where Sherman's promise of "40 acres and a mule" was snatched back.

The consequences were long-lasting. Barbados hardened into one of the most rigid **plantation class societies**[16] in the Caribbean, with a tiny white elite dominating politics, land, and wealth while the Black majority remained trapped in cycles of sugar-based dependency. This inequality festered into the 20th century, erupting in the **1937 labor riots,** when cane cutters and urban workers rose against poverty wages and colonial neglect. The riots forced reforms but also spotlighted the unfinished business of emancipation.

Today, that demand echoes louder than ever. Barbados's Prime Minister **Mia Mottley** has placed reparations at the heart of her agenda, aligning with CARICOM's collective call for justice. Estimates suggest Britain owes as much as **£3.9 trillion** for the extraction, underdevelopment, and generational poverty produced by slavery. For Barbados, where sugar once built fortunes for London while leaving Black laborers landless and impoverished, reparations are not charity they are the repayment of a debt centuries overdue.

False Freedoms, Enduring Chains

In the Bahamas, Haiti, and Barbados, and across the wider Caribbean the end of slavery was less a revolution than a rebranding. Britain's apprenticeship, France's indemnity, and sharecropping contracts in "Little England" all proved the same truth: colonial powers knew how to extract wealth even in defeat, ensuring that emancipation served empire more than it served the emancipated. The chains were never truly broken, only reshaped.

16 Plantation Society: Post-1834, a white elite controlled land and politics, trapping the Black majority in sugar-based poverty via sharecropping and truck systems.

These Caribbean betrayals mirror the U.S. South's enduring traps: **sharecropping that replaced slavery with debt peonage, Jim Crow laws that stripped political voice, and disenfranchisement that rendered freedom hollow.** Across the diaspora, Black labor built nations, but Black ownership was systematically denied. The soil that bore sugar, cotton, rice, and indigo was never returned to those whose sweat consecrated it.

And yet, survival became culture. Junkanoo in the Bahamas, Emancipation Day parades in Barbados (Crop Over), Vodou drumming in Haiti all emerged as acts of resilience, cultural defiance against systems designed to erase. These traditions remind us that though bodies were bound, spirits endured, and memory kept the flame alive.

But the struggle did not end in 1834 or 1804. It continues today in the **global reparations movement,** which demands repayment for centuries of theft; in the cries for land reform, economic equity, and sovereignty; and in the simple declaration that freedom without ownership is still a form of servitude. From the Bahamian cays to the Haitian hills, from Barbadian cane fields to Carolina swamps, the call remains the same: **true freedom means land, legacy, and self-determination.**

Until that reckoning is made, the descendants of the enslaved continue to labor sustaining economic systems never designed for their freedom. Survival has too often been mistaken for progress, endurance for justice. The structures that once enforced bondage land denial, debt, and exclusion were never dismantled, only renamed and inherited. The unfinished task before us is not remembrance alone, but completion: to confront the economic afterlife of slavery and to secure a future where freedom is measured not by how long one can endure, but by sovereignty, ownership, dignity, and self-determination.

Chapter 4

BLOODLINES ACROSS THE SEA, LINKING THE CAROLINAS AND THE BAHAMAS

The waters between the Carolinas and The Bahamas are more than a geographical divide; they are a living artery of shared blood, sweat, and spirit. Across these currents traveled Loyalist exiles, slave ships, and fugitives alike carrying with them not only people, but cultures, traumas, and traditions that stitched two worlds into one. Long before leisure and luxury, this passage functioned as what might be called the first **Caribbean Cruise** one powered by forced migration, survival, and empire rather than choice.

When the American Revolution fractured the South, loyalists fled Charleston, Savannah, and the Georgia coast, towing thousands of enslaved Africans to the Bahamas and its family islands. These men, women, and children were not strangers to the soil or the sea. They were Gullah-Geechee[17] kin, bearers of languages rooted in West Africa, of rice-growing expertise, of spiritual practices that remembered drums even when drums were banned. Their exile did not sever bloodlines it replanted them, weaving a bridge across the Atlantic tide that linked the Carolina Lowcountry to Bahamian cays.

That bridge endures. In the call-and-response of Bahamian Junkanoo, one hears echoes of Gullah ring shouts. In the shared surnames Johnson, Rolle, Pinder, Sweeting one traces the stamp of Loyalist slavery and African recaptives. In foodways, peas 'n' rice mirrors Carolina red rice, while okra stews and conch fritters tell of an African palate remixed in new waters. Even the cadence of speech, the rolling rhythms of Bahamian Creole and the lilting tones of Gullah-Geechee testify to a common root system stretching from Sierra Leone and Senegal to Charleston and Nassau.

However, these bloodlines also carry chains, as well as culture. They remind us of labor without ownership: rice, indigo, and cotton in the Carolinas; cotton, salt, and pineapples in the Bahamas. They remind us of survival without sovereignty: free in name yet bound to colonial economies that paid nothing for centuries of toil. "From can't see to can't see" was not just a Southern phrase, it was an island refrain, sung by those who rose before dawn to rake salt or dive sponges and returned only after the stars reclaimed the sky.

To trace these connections is to see more than history, it is to glimpse a blueprint for the future a blueprint for reclamation. For if the same bloodlines carried chains, they also carried culture, resilience, and memory. The Gullah-Geechee and Bahamian people stand today not as fractured descendants, but as living proof of diaspora unbroken. Their survival sketches the path forward: to reclaim land, legacy, and ownership on both sides of the sea.

17 Gullah-Geechee: African American communities in SC, GA, NC, and FL, descended from enslaved Africans, preserving West African language, culture, and spiritual practices.

Loyalist Migration from the Carolinas to the Bahamas (1780s)

The American Revolution shattered empires and scattered lives, propelling a wave of British Loyalists from the Carolinas southward to the Bahamas in the 1780s an exodus born of defeat, desperation, and the Crown's hollow promises. When the Treaty of Paris[18] ended the war in 1783, thousands of

18 Treaty of Paris (1783): Ended the American Revolution, granting U.S. independence and prompting British Loyalists, including South Carolina and North Carolina planters, to flee to the Bahamas with enslaved Gullah-Geechee, reinforcing the plantation class society.

white Loyalists many from South Carolina's elite rice and indigo planters in Charleston and the lowcountry, as well as families from North Carolina's Cape Fear and Wilmington regions fled persecution in the new United States. For their loyalty to Britain, they were branded traitors by the patriots; their lands were confiscated, their fortunes lost.

The British solution was exile. Promised land grants and "fresh starts" in the Caribbean, Loyalists boarded ships with families, possessions, and most importantly their enslaved labor force. Between 5,000 and 8,000 Loyalists arrived in the Bahamas, accompanied by an estimated 6,000-9,000 enslaved Africans, effectively doubling the islands' population almost overnight. Islands like New Providence, Abaco, Eleuthera, and Cat Island became new frontiers for Loyalist ambitions, their forests cleared and soil pressed into cotton, sisal, and provision farming.

For the enslaved Africans, this migration meant chains transplanted from the rice swamps of Carolina to the rocky limestone of the Bahamian islands and cays. They carried with them not only labor but also memory: the Gullah-Geechee rhythms of language, knowledge of rice cultivation, crafts such as basket-weaving, and spiritual traditions that had survived in coded prayers and songs. These cultural threads stitched the Bahamas into the wider African Atlantic fabric, leaving legacies still visible in speech, food, and family names.

The Loyalists, meanwhile, recreated a society as stratified as the one they left. They imported Carolina's slave codes into Bahamian law, entrenching racial hierarchy and economic dependence. Their surnames Rolle, Pinder, Johnson, Minns, Curry, Sweeting still echo across the islands today, borne both by descendants of enslavers and of the enslaved.

This migration was more than relocation; it was the transplantation of the Carolinas' plantation economy and social order into Bahamian soil. The waters between Nassau and Charleston thus became not a divide but a bridge, binding two societies through shared bloodlines, forced labor, and cultural survival.

The Loyalist Peak (1783–1785): Transplanting Carolina into Bahamian Soil

Figure 20 Colonel Andrew Deveaux (30 April 1758 – 11 July 1812) was an American Loyalist from South Carolina who is most famous for his recapture of the Bahamas in 1783.

This migration peaked between 1783 and 1785, when more than 7,000 Loyalists flooded into the Bahamian islands, many sailing from East Florida, a short-lived Loyalist refuge ceded back to Spain. Southerners from Georgia and the Carolinas comprised nearly 70% of these newcomers, accompanied by thousands of enslaved Africans who had already endured the grind of rice and indigo fields. The demographic shift was seismic: in just two years, Nassau transformed from a fading pirate outpost into a bustling Loyalist enclave, its narrow streets suddenly crowded with planters, merchants, and the enslaved who bore their wealth on bent backs.

Figures like Colonel Andrew Deveaux, a South Carolina Loyalist, embodied this new order. In 1783, Deveaux led a daring expedition of Loyalist privateers and enslaved laborers to wrest the islands from Spanish control, securing them firmly for Britain. His victory symbolized the Loyalists' determination not merely to survive but to rebuild the plantation society they had lost on the mainland.

Plantations soon appeared across the Out Islands. On Exuma, Long Island, Cat Island, and Eleuthera, Loyalists planted sea island cotton a crop requiring intensive hand labor, from clearing coral rock fields to delicately harvesting lint. They also turned to salt production in Inagua and Exuma, where enslaved Africans raked crystallized salt from pans under a blistering sun, their bare feet eaten raw by brine. The Loyalists imported Carolina's plantation codes, discipline, and slave laws wholesale, ensuring that the old order lived on in new soil.

Yet the soil itself rebelled. Unlike the fertile rice swamps of Carolina, Bahamian limestone was thin, porous, and prone to drought. Cotton fields withered, pests devoured crops, and yields fell far short of Carolina expectations. Many Loyalist fortunes collapsed within a generation, leaving the enslaved still chained but their master's increasingly impoverished. In this failure lay the irony of Loyalist migration: they carried Carolina's system across the sea, but the Bahamas could not sustain it.

What endured was not wealth, but legacy. The surnames of these Loyalist settlers, Rolle, Deveaux, Curry, Johnson, Minns, and Pinder still mark Bahamian families today, borne by both descendants of planters and the enslaved who once labored under them. Their arrival embedded Carolina's bloodlines, culture, and oppression into Bahamian life, binding the Lowcountry and the islands in a shared story of transplantation, survival, and unfinished freedom.

Loyalist Architecture, Governance, and Ideology in the Bahamas

Yet, this "favorable terms" migration—subsidized by the Crown through land grants, stipends, and transport— Figure 21 The Loyalist Cottage Built in 1797

masked the actual human cost: Loyalists brought not only their families but their "property," ensuring slavery's transplant across the sea. Within a decade, the Bahamas' population tripled, reshaping the islands from scattered outposts into a structured slave society. By 1790, enslaved

Africans made up most of the population, echoing the demographic imbalance of the Carolinas and cementing the Bahamas as another link in Britain's plantation empire.

The influence of the Carolinas was visible everywhere. In architecture, Loyalists recreated the Lowcountry in wood and limestone, featuring steep-roofed clapboard cottages with dormer windows, wide verandas, and louvered shutters such as the Loyalist Cottage on Harbor Island, built in 1797 that still stand as symbols of transplanted Southern culture. In governance, Loyalists reshaped the colonial assembly, embedding planter-dominated politics that mirrored South Carolina's House of Commons, ensuring that wealth and race dictated power. Nassau's streets, its Anglican churches, and its plantation layouts all bore the stamp of Charleston and Savannah, transported wholesale across the waves.

But this was no mere relocation, it was a lifeline for Loyalist ideology. By bringing slavery with them, Loyalists seeded the islands with southern hierarchies that perpetuated racial control long after emancipation. The apprenticeship system of the 1830s, the truck wages of the sponge trade, and even modern class divides in the Bahamas all trace their roots to this Loyalist migration.

This maritime corridor forged a shared destiny that still shapes the present. The economic logics, racial hierarchies, and labor expectations carried across these waters did not dissolve with emancipation or independence; they settled into law, culture, and memory on both shores. What emerged was a transatlantic inheritance, one in which freedom was promised but postponed, mobility existed without security, and labor remained extractive. To understand this passage is to understand that the struggle for justice in the Caribbean and the American South has never been isolated but interconnected bound by the same tides that once carried chains and now carry the unfinished work of repair.

Enslaved Africans Brought Along, Creating a Genetic and Cultural Bridge

Figure 22 1770s ships like the Lord Dunmore or Peace and Plenty

No migration is complete without its shadows, and the Loyalists' exodus carried the weight of thousands of enslaved Africans,human cargo uprooted from Carolina soil and cast onto Bahamian sands. Estimates suggest between 4,000 and 6,000 enslaved people accompanied their Loyalist masters, outnumbering whites and instantly transforming the Bahamas into a Black-majority society. These men, women, and children skilled artisans, seasoned field hands, and domestic workers were treated as movable property, loaded onto ships like the Lord Dunmore or Peace and Plenty with no promise of freedom, only new chains in unfamiliar islands.

Figure 23 Beautiful Baskets of Heritage, Made by the Gullah Weavers

Upon arrival in Abaco, Exuma, and New Providence, they were set to work clearing dense brush and coral rock to plant cotton repeating the "from can't see to can't see" rhythm of toil they had known in Carolina rice swamps. Others turned to salt raking on Long Island, sponge diving in Andros, or wreck salvaging along the treacherous Bahamian reefs, laboring in industries just as grueling as those of the plantation fields. The economic foundations of the islands, whether cotton, salt, or maritime trades rested squarely on their backs.

Yet in their suffering, they carried and preserved African-descended traditions that stitched a cultural bridge across the sea. Gullah-Geechee echoes from the Carolinas blended with Yoruba and Igbo survivals, pulsing through Bahamian speech, basket weaving, storytelling, drumming, and song. The African majority reshaped the Bahamas from within, ensuring that while Loyalists brought their hierarchies, it was African resilience that gave the islands their living soul. This genetic and cultural bridge spanning Charleston's tidal marshes and Nassau's harbor, Carolina's sea islands and Exuma's cays remains visible today in the names, foods, and rhythms that bind the diaspora.

Figure 24 Straw Basket made by Bahamian Weavers

Genetically and Culturally Bound Across the Sea

Genetically, the bridge between the Carolinas and the Bahamas is inscribed in DNA itself. Modern genetic studies reveal shared ancestry markers among Bahamians and Gullah-Geechee descendants, with roots in West and Central Africa carried across the Atlantic on the same slave routes. Surnames like Rolle, Bethel, Johnson, and Smith common across both regions, testify to these transplants, often traceable to specific Carolina households. These names, stripped from African identities and imposed by colonial owners, nevertheless became vessels linking kin separated by sea.

Culturally, the enslaved carried far more than chains they bore intangible treasures of survival and resilience. Creole languages, African spiritualities, and agricultural skills crossed the water with them, blending with the remnants of Indigenous Arawak traditions to create hybrid cultures still alive today. Carolina's Gullah basketry mirrors Bahamian straw plaiting; ring shouts on the South Carolina coast echo in the rhythms of Junkanoo; spiritual systems like hoodoo and obeah reflect a shared African cosmology reshaped under the conditions of slavery. This forced migration was not simply a relocation of bodies it wove a transatlantic tapestry where memory survived oppression, carried in music, craft, story, and spirit.

Across generations, bloodlines and traditions continued to speak when written records fell silent. What slavery tried to fragment, memory reassembled through shared rhythms, crafts, beliefs, and kinship ties that defied the ocean meant to separate them. The sea did not sever these people from one another; it bound them. In this way, the Carolinas and the Bahamas remain linked not only by history, but by an unbroken inheritance of survival, identity, and remembrance.

Tribal Roots: Gola, Yoruba, Mende, and Akan

The bloodlines binding the Carolinas and The Bahamas trace to deep African wellsprings particularly the **Gola** and **Mende** of Sierra Leone and Liberia, the **Yoruba** of Nigeria, and the **Akan** of Ghana's **Ashanti** and Fante states. These people were disproportionately targeted in the slave trade, feeding both regions, precisely because their expertise made them "valuable" commodities.

- **Gola and Mende:** Masters of rice cultivation, they fueled Carolina's "gold crop" economy and brought subsistence knowledge to Bahamian soils. Their poro and sande secret societies left cultural imprints in their initiation rituals, which were echoed in Gullah hoodoo and Bahamian obeah.
- **Yoruba:** Their orisha traditions infused diasporic spiritual life, leaving traces in ring shouts, Junkanoo drumming, and even creole vocabulary "buckra" (white person) has Yoruba roots. Yoruba cosmology reinforced communal resistance, shaping survival strategies across both regions.
- **Akan:** Renowned goldsmiths and warriors, the Akan transmitted craftsmanship and matrilineal kinship structures. Family organization, proverbs, and folklore in both Gullah tales and Bahamian storytelling carry Akan DNA in cultural form.

Genetic studies confirm these origins: haplogroups like **L1b** (Mende/ Gola) and **E1b1a** (Yoruba/Akan) appear with high frequency among both Gullah and Bahamian descendants, linking modern identities to ancestors kidnapped from ports like Ouidah and Freetown. Loyalist migrations in the 1780s amplified these bonds, transplanting enslaved Africans already seasoned in Carolina's fields into Bahamian cotton and salt industries.

Reclaiming Origins

Today, these tribal echoes fuel cultural revivals from Gullah festivals in South Carolina to Junkanoo in Nassau. They remind us that identity was never erased, only buried beneath colonial names and systems of bondage. Reclamation begins with recognizing that our heritage is not fractured, but shared a single river with many branches, flowing from Africa's shores to the Carolinas' marshes to the Bahamas' islands and cays. Ownership of history begins with reclaiming these roots, restoring dignity to the ancestors who turned exile into endurance.

Shared Cultural Remnants: Gullah-Geechee, Bush Medicine, and Storytelling

The deepest legacies of survival live in culture. Across the Carolinas and the Bahamas, African-descended people wove memories into daily life, preserving fragments of their identity through speech, medicine, and storytelling.

Language: The Gullah-Geechee creole of the Carolina Sea Islands shares striking similarities with Bahamian dialects, both of which were formed from African languages adapted to English under plantation regimes. Their cadence, intonation, and word choice mirror one another, so much so that linguists and everyday people alike note how "they sound alike." Phrases like "day clean" for dawn are not coincidences they are survival codes carried across the Atlantic, whispered by ancestors and kept alive through generations.

Bush Medicine, Storytelling, and Festivals as Acts of Survival

Figure 25 Gullah Festival 30th year heritage

Bush medicine, rooted in Akan and Yoruba herbal traditions, remains one of the diaspora's most enduring inheritances. In the Carolinas, root doctors prescribed sassafras to break fevers and conjure strength, while in the Bahamas, elders brewed bush teas from cerasee, five-finger, love-vine, or life everlasting. These remedies were not merely cures for the body, they were knowledge carried in whispers, passed hand to hand to defy colonial bans and preserve an African science that refused to die.

Storytelling was another medicine. The Mende and Gola carried folktales across the Atlantic, where they resurfaced as Gullah tales of Br'er Rabbit outwitting stronger foes and Bahamian porchside stories of Br'er Bucky and Br'er Rabby. To children, they were entertainment; to adults, they were survival manuals reminding the oppressed that wit, patience, and solidarity could outlast the lash. Even figures like the Gullah "hag" or Bahamian "jumbee" embodied lessons about vigilance and resilience.

Festivals sealed this memory in sound and spectacle. Junkanoo in The Bahamas and the Ring Shout in the Carolinas carried Africa into the New World through rhythm, masks, and dance. Drums beat not just for celebration, but for survival summoning ancestors, mocking masters, and declaring that African identity was unbroken.

These remnants are not relics. They are tools of healing and resistance, urging us to reclaim narrative, land, and legacy. From the rice marshes of Carolina to the cays of The Bahamas, the bloodlines of survival call for ownership not just of memory, but of futures. To break the "can't see to can't see" grind is to finish the work our ancestors began: to turn endurance into liberation.

What sustained these communities was not nostalgia, but strategy. Knowledge had to be hidden in plain sight, coded into songs, prayers, recipes, jokes, and rituals that appeared harmless to overseers but carried instruction and memory beneath the surface. Survival depended on adaptability: knowing when to speak, when to silence oneself, when to gather, and when to scatter. Culture became armor, and memory became a map.

These practices also created continuity where records were erased. When names, languages, and homelands were stolen, people rebuilt lineage through shared habits and beliefs. A plant used for healing, a story told at dusk, a drumbeat carried through the night all became ways of remembering who one was in a world designed to make forgetting inevitable. In this way, culture replaced what law and history denied.

Yet resilience alone was never the end goal. These traditions were born not to romanticize suffering, but to outlive it. They carried within them an unfinished demand: that survival must eventually give way to security, ownership, and self-determination. Healing without justice is incomplete, and memory without material repair risks becoming another burden placed on the descendants of the enslaved.

To honor these inheritances is therefore not only to preserve them, but to act on what they point toward. From bush medicine to storytelling, from festival to faith, the message is consistent: endurance was only the beginning. Breaking the "can't see to can't see" cycle requires finishing the work our ancestors could not transforming survival into sovereignty, culture into power, and inherited struggle into inherited freedom.

PART TWO

AFTER EMANCIPATION, STILL IN BONDAGE

Chapter 5

THE PROMISE THAT NEVER CAME

Emancipation rang across the Atlantic like a great bell, its echoes rolling from Haiti in 1804, to the British Caribbean in 1834, to the United States in 1865. To the enslaved and newly freed, it sounded like a summons to a new world land for the landless, wages for the robbed, and dignity for those long stripes of it. For a moment, the horizon glowed with possibility: ownership, autonomy, and the chance to live as human beings rather than as property.

But when the bell's echoes faded, silence revealed betrayal promises dissolved like mist in the sun. In the United States, "forty acres and a mule" was revoked, leaving freedmen in the Carolinas tethered to the land as sharecroppers. In the British Caribbean, apprenticeship replaced slavery in name only, binding the emancipated to their former masters' fields without pay or property. Even Haiti, born of revolution, was shackled by France's crushing indemnity debt, forcing a nation of freed people to pay reparations to their enslavers.

Freedom was declared, but bondage was redesigned. The whip became the wage, overseers became creditors, and the plantation system morphed into a lattice of contracts, vagrancy laws, and exploitative economies that locked Black communities in cycles of toil without reward. Across Charleston's rice swamps, Nassau's cotton patches, and Haiti's mountain farms, the refrain was the same: **"From can't see to can't see" did not end,it simply changed its overseer.**

These betrayals were not accidents of history; they were engineered absences carefully crafted voids of land, wealth, and power meant to ensure that generations would grind without gain. To name them is not to despair but to defy. By unearthing these broken promises, we reclaim the vision of building the freedom our ancestors were denied, forging a future rooted not in scraps from an empire, but in the sovereignty of our own making.

What was withheld at emancipation was not accidental neglect but deliberate design. Land was denied because land confers power; capital was restricted because capital enables independence; political voice was constrained because voice disrupts control. Across the Atlantic world, freedom was carefully rationed to ensure that labor remained abundant, cheap, and disciplined. The result was a shared inheritance of struggle one that demands not gratitude for partial freedom, but insistence on its completion. To reckon honestly with emancipation is to acknowledge that liberation delayed is liberation denied, and that the work of transforming freedom from promise into possession remains unfinished.

The Betrayal of 40 Acres, a Mule, and Seeds

No symbol exposes emancipation's hollow core more clearly than the broken promise of "40 acres, a mule, and seeds." It was not just land, it was the key to autonomy, wealth, and survival. In 1865, Union General William T. Sherman's Special Field Order No. 15 pledged formerly enslaved families' plots carved from confiscated Confederate estates. For a brief, shining moment, thousands of freedmen in Georgia and the Carolinas believed justice might finally take root in soil they could call their own.

But within months, President Andrew Johnson rescinded the order, restoring land to former Confederate owners and expelling freed people who had already begun to farm it. What had been promised as the foundation of independence was replaced with a system of sharecropping, debt peonage, and labor contracts designed to keep Black families tied to white landowners. Instead of sovereignty, they inherited servitude under a new name.

This betrayal was not simply a political reversal it was a generational theft. Land ownership is the cornerstone of wealth, yet Black Americans were deliberately denied it at the very moment it was most within reach. Meanwhile, planters received forgiveness, subsidies, and, in some cases, compensation for their "losses." Freed people were left with nothing but their labor, forced once again to grind without reward.

The echoes of that broken promise still resonate today in the form of wealth gaps, land dispossession, and ongoing struggles for reparations. "Forty acres and a mule" remains not just a slogan, but a haunting reminder of what could have been a vision of justice stolen at the very threshold of freedom.

The Birth of a Promise

Figure 26 General William T. Sherman's Courtest of U.S National Archives

The pledge of "forty acres and a mule" emerged from the crucible of the Civil War, forged in the ashes of rebellion and the cries for justice. On January 16, 1865, Union General William T. Sherman issued **Special Field Orders No. 15** after his infamous March to the Sea, which had left Confederate strongholds smoldering. Meeting with a council of Black ministers and community leaders in Savannah, Sherman did something radical: he listened. Their demand was clear, land, not charity.

Sherman's order carved out 400,000 acres of confiscated Confederate plantations along the coasts of South Carolina, Georgia, and Florida fertile rice and cotton lands that had once enriched the very men who fought to keep slavery alive. For the first time, justice seemed to move beyond words: freed families were to receive up to **40 acres each,** and surplus army mules would be provided to till the soil.

By June 1865, more than 40,000 freedmen had taken root on this land, from Edisto Island in South Carolina to Skidaway Island in Georgia. They built cabins, planted fields, and built schools and churches. Under the Freedmen's Bureau, established that March, titles were issued, and for a brief, radiant moment, Black autonomy flourished on the very soil that had once shackled their ancestors.

This was more than land redistribution, it was reparative justice, a vision of transformation where centuries of unpaid toil would finally yield independence. For those months, the dream of dignity seemed tangible: a future where formerly enslaved people could live as freeholders, secure in the fruits of their own labor.

The Great Betrayal

Figure 27 President Andrew Johnson 1870

The dream of landownership was shattered almost as quickly as it was born. After President Abraham Lincoln's assassination in April 1865, his successor, **Andrew Johnson**, a Southern Democrat with deep sympathies for ex-Confederates, chose reconciliation with white planters over justice for freed people.

By the fall of 1865, Johnson issued sweeping pardons to Confederate landowners and ordered the restoration of their estates. Families who had already cleared fields, built cabins, and planted crops under Sherman's orders were suddenly branded squatters on land they had been promised. U.S. troops were dispatched to enforce evictions.

On South Carolina's Sea Islands, where Gullah communities had flourished in their brief autonomy, freed people protested in desperation:

"This is our home. We have made these lands what they are."

But their petitions were ignored. By 1866, most of the 400,000 acres once promised to freed families were back in the hands of the very men who had enslaved them.

Stripped of title and leverage, Black families were forced into **sharecropping and tenant farming,** renting small plots from white landlords at crushing rates. Bound by debt, cheated in harvest settlements, and tied to land they could never own, they found themselves trapped in a cycle of servitude **slavery by another name.**

The consequences reverberate still. Economists estimate that the loss of "forty acres" represents **over $326 billion in unrealized Black wealth,** wealth that could have secured generational stability. In the Carolinas, where rice fields once held the promise of freedom, Black labor returned to the same rhythm of exploitation "from can't see to can't see" only now under contracts instead of chains.

This was no accident of history. It was a **deliberate act of sabotage against Black economic independence,** ensuring that emancipation would ring hollow. The betrayal of land redistribution in the United States mirrors the Caribbean's own failures after emancipation: freedom declared, but ownership denied.

The denial of land was the denial of a future. Without ownership, freedom was stripped of its substance and reduced to survival within systems designed by former enslavers. Sharecropping, debt, and legal coercion ensured that Black labor remained productive while Black autonomy remained impossible. Emancipation offered release from chains, but not release from control.

This great betrayal binds the United States to the Caribbean in a shared aftermath of broken promises. Across the Atlantic world, freedom was proclaimed while power was withheld, ensuring that generations would labor without legacy. The work left unfinished is clear: until land, wealth, and self-determination are restored, emancipation remains incomplete, and "can't see to can't see" endures as both memory and mandate.

RECONSTRUCTION FAILURES IN THE U.S.

Figure 28"Robert Smalls, S.C. M.C. Born in Beaufort, SC, April 1839.

Reconstruction's Flickering Flame

Reconstruction (1865–1877) glowed like a fragile flame briefly illuminating a path to equality before being snuffed out by violence and betrayal. For the first time in American history, Black citizenship, political power, and economic independence seemed possible. But in the Carolinas, where the promise shone brightest, its collapse cut deepest.

The victories were monumental. The **13th Amendment (1865)** abolished slavery; the **14th (1868)** guaranteed citizenship and equal protection; and the **15th (1870)** secured voting rights for Black men. South Carolina became a beacon: Black legislators, such as Robert Smalls, a former enslaved man who went on to become a Civil War hero, filled the state assembly, championing public education, fair taxation, and land reform. Freedmen founded farms, schools, and churches; the Freedmen's Bureau distributed rations, built schools, and defended civil rights. For a fleeting moment, democracy in the South looked truly multiracial.

Yet progress bred backlash. President Andrew Johnson's leniency restored political power to ex-Confederates, who quickly drafted **Black Codes**[19] to shackle freedom. These laws barred Black people from owning property, freely contracting labor, or moving without papers. **Vagrancy laws** criminalized unemployment, forcing freedmen into exploitative labor contracts that resembled slavery in all but name.

Radical Republicans in Congress tried to strike back, imposing military Reconstruction and expanding protections, but enforcement faltered as Northern resolve waned. White vigilante groups like the **Ku Klux Klan** unleashed terror, lynchings, arson, and massacres to crush Black political participation. Ballot boxes were stuffed or stolen, gunfire silenced elections. By the late 1870s, "Redemption" governments restored white supremacy, dismantling Black-led reforms.

Reconstruction had promised land, law, and liberty. Instead, freed families in the Carolinas found themselves pushed back into **sharecropping and debt peonage,** hemmed in by violence and stripped of rights they had briefly held. The dream of freedom survived, but only as a memory carried in song, prayer, and whispered determination.

19. Black Codes were laws enacted in Southern states after the Civil War to restrict the freedom and rights of African Americans, enforcing labor control and segregation.

THE HAMBURG RIOT, JULY, 1876

Reconstruction's Violent Undoing

If Reconstruction flickered as a fragile flame, terrorism and betrayal were the winds that snuffed it out. White supremacist groups like the **Ku Klux Klan** and the **Red Shirts** waged open warfare against Black freedom, using destructive behavior to intimidate and silence voters and leaders. South Carolina became the crucible of this counterrevolution: the **Hamburg Massacre of 1876**[20]**,** where white paramilitaries slaughtered Black militiamen, signaled the death knell of Black political power. Across the South, such massacres were not anomalies, but strategies terror deployed as policy to "redeem" the South for white Democrats.

20 The Hamburg Massacre of 1876 was a violent racial attack in Hamburg, South Carolina, where white paramilitaries killed at least six Black militia members after a dispute, escalating Reconstruction-era tensions.

The betrayal was sealed in Washington. The **Compromise of 1877**[21] a backroom deal to resolve a contested presidential election traded away Black rights for white reconciliation. Federal troops withdrew from the South, leaving freed people defenseless against violence and stripping Reconstruction governments of their only protection. Within a decade, Jim **Crow**[22] was entrenched: poll taxes, literacy tests, and grandfather clauses disenfranchised over 90% of Black voters by 1900, erasing the gains of the 14th and 15th Amendments.

Economics proved no kinder. Without land reform, freed families were trapped in **sharecropping,** forced to rent land from former enslavers in exchange for a portion of their harvest. **Crop lien laws**[23] ensured that debt rolled from year to year, tethering generations to perpetual poverty. In the Carolinas, where Black communities had once envisioned independence in the rice and cotton fields, the dream of landownership was buried beneath contracts designed to mimic slavery.

For many, the only escape was flight. The **Great Migration** carried hundreds of thousands northward, away from the horrors of lynching and debt peonage, toward factories and railroads that promised opportunity but delivered new forms of exploitation simply shifted from the cotton rows of the South to the steel mills of Pittsburgh and the slaughterhouses of Chicago.

Reconstruction did not fail by accident; it was **sabotaged by design.** The nation chose white unity over Black justice, leaving the descendants of the enslaved bound in poverty and violence. The wealth gap, voter suppression, and systemic racism that plague America today are not broken promises, they are the direct inheritance of a Reconstruction deliberately destroyed.

21 The Compromise of 1877 was an unwritten agreement that resolved the disputed 1876 presidential election by awarding Republican Rutherford B. Hayes the presidency in exchange for withdrawing federal troops from the South, effectively ending Reconstruction and enabling Southern states to impose discriminatory laws against African Americans.

22 Jim Crow refers to a system of state and local laws enacted in the late 19th and early 20th centuries in the Southern United States to enforce racial segregation and disenfranchise African Americans, perpetuating systemic inequality until the Civil Rights Movement.

23 Crop lien laws were post-Civil War statutes in Southern states that allowed merchants and landowners to place liens on farmers' crops, often trapping sharecroppers, particularly African Americans, in cycles of debt and economic dependency.

No Land, No Freedom: Caribbean Betrayals

Across the Atlantic, emancipation in the Caribbean unfolded with the same cruel irony as in the Carolinas: slavery was abolished, yet freedom was stripped of its foundation land. Without land reform, the newly emancipated remained tethered to colonial elites, foreign creditors, and exploitative economies, condemned to a freedom that looked much like bondage.

In the **British Caribbean,** emancipation in 1834 arrived shackled to the so-called "apprenticeship" system: a period of four to six years of unpaid labor, ensuring planters squeezed profit from Black hands even after the chains fell. When the apprenticeship ended in 1838, freedom rang hollow. Crown lands remained in white planter control, while freed people were herded into wage tenancy, sharecropping, and exploitative contracts. In the **Bahamas,** they raked salt in blistering sun or scratched at exhausted cotton soils, while elites held title to fertile lands. In **Jamaica,** this hunger for land erupted in the **Morant Bay Rebellion of 1865**[24]**,** when Black peasants, starving and dispossessed rose in protest. Britain's response was brutal: martial law, villages torched, hundreds executed. The message was clear land belonged to the empire, not to those who had earned it in blood. Compensation, like in the Carolinas, flowed only to enslavers: Britain's £20 million reparations to planters enriched elites, while the enslaved received nothing but poverty and debt.

24 The Morant Bay Rebellion of 1865 was an uprising in Jamaica led by Baptist preacher Paul Bogle, where hundreds of Black protesters marched on the Morant Bay courthouse to protest economic hardships, land disputes, and legal injustices, resulting in the burning of the building, the deaths of at least 18 officials, and a brutal colonial suppression that executed over 400 Black Jamaicans and ended Jamaican self-government.

Haiti's path was different, yet equally shackled. Having won independence through revolution in 1804 the only successful slave revolt in history Haiti outlawed slavery forever. But in 1825, France returned with warships and extortion, demanding **150 million francs** for its "losses." This ransom, reduced to 90 million but financed by predatory French loans, drained Haiti for over a century, paid in full only in 1947. Instead of building schools, roads, and local industries, Haiti's wealth was siphoned to its former enslavers. Land was redistributed under Dessalines, broken into peasant plots and **lakou** compounds, but without capital or credit, peasants remained vulnerable to famine, hurricanes, and foreign interference. Later
U.S. occupation (1915–1934) reinforced elite dominance, ensuring that ownership remained out of reach for the masses.

Across the Caribbean specifically, the Bahamas, Jamaica, Barbados, and Haiti, the story repeats: freedom without land, liberty without ownership, and **survival without sovereignty.** Where the Carolinas offered "40 acres and a mule" only to snatch it away, the Caribbean promised emancipation but denied land, embedding dependency on sugar, cotton, and later tourism. Both systems ensured that Black labor fueled the empire while Black families inherited only exhaustion.

Yet, in naming this betrayal, we reclaim its lessons. Land is more than soil; it is freedom, legacy, and future. The unkept promises of the 19th century must fuel today's demand for reparations, for ownership, for true emancipation. Only when we seize what was withheld can we finally end the cycle of grinding.

Across the Caribbean, emancipation without land proved to be freedom in name only. Whether through Britain's apprenticeship schemes, planter control of crown lands, violent repression of land-hungry peasants, or France's extortion of revolutionary Haiti, the pattern was consistent: ownership was denied preserving empire. Black labor remained essential, but Black independence was treated as a threat. To confront this betrayal is to affirm a simple truth, land is not merely property, but the foundation of freedom, and until it is restored, the grind of "can't see to can't see" remains unfinished history rather than past wrong.

Chapter 6

SHARECROPPING, INDENTURE, AND ECONOMIC TRAPS

"These were not mere policy failures but deliberate tools of empire, keeping Black freedom a faint shadow rather than a reality. To reclaim time, land, and vision, we must confront the unbroken chains of economic exploitation stretching from Carolina cotton fields to Caribbean cane brakes, empowering descendants to build the ownership, sovereignty, and rest long denied."

Emancipation's ink had barely dried when new shackles emerged subtler than iron but no less binding. Across the Carolinas and the Caribbean, freedom morphed into facsimile bondage through economic traps engineered to extract labor without granting ownership. These systems **sharecropping in the U.S. South, indenture and apprenticeship in the Caribbean** did not merely sustain poverty; they institutionalized it, ensuring Black and brown families toiled "from can't see to can't see" for generations. Sweat-enriched landlords, planters, and empires, while those who worked the land inherited only exhaustion and lack.

Sharecropping in the Carolinas

In the aftermath of the Civil War, landless freed people in the Carolinas were lured into sharecropping contracts. Promised a share of the harvest in exchange for labor, they quickly found the system was rigged. White landlords and merchants controlled the prices of seeds, tools, and even food often advancing them on credit through the **crop lien system**. At harvest time, debts always outweighed earnings, binding families to a perpetual state of servitude. Sharecrops lived in fear of eviction, violence, or fabricated debts that carried from one year to the next, trapping generations in cycles of dependence.

Worse still, the system stripped autonomy: planters dictated what crops had to be grown, prioritizing cotton or rice for profit rather than subsistence food. Freed families remained hungry, indebted, and dispossessed working the same fields their ancestors had, but now under contracts instead of chains. In practice, sharecropping was slavery reinvented, its cruel efficiency evident in the fact that by 1900, the majority of Black farmers in the South still owned no land, despite decades of backbreaking labor.

These systems were not failures of transition but successes of design. By replacing chains with contracts and overseers with creditors, post-emancipation economies preserved the core function of slavery while shedding its name. Labor remained compulsory, mobility constrained, and ownership perpetually out of reach. Across fields once tilled in bondage, freedom demanded the same endless exertion with none of the promised rewards. In this way, "can't see to can't see" survived emancipation, not as a relic of the past, but as a living structure that disciplined Black labor long after slavery's legal end.

Indenture and Apprenticeship in the Caribbean

The Caribbean, under British and French colonial rule, offered no greater reprieve. The **apprenticeship system (1834–1838)**[25] in colonies like Jamaica, Barbados, and the Bahamas extended slavery in disguise. Freed men and women were forced to work unpaid for their former masters up to 45 hours per week, their "freedom" reduced to a legal fiction. Punishments whippings, imprisonment, loss of wages, remained as tools of control, while planters consolidated land and influence.

After the apprenticeship ended, the vacuum was filled with another system of bondage: **indentured servitude.** Colonial governments imported hundreds of thousands of Indian, Chinese, and Portuguese laborers under harsh contracts to replace enslaved Africans. These indentured workers endured brutal hours, low pay, and debt that kept them bound to plantations for years, often overlapping with and undermining the economic prospects of the emancipated Black majority. Meanwhile, formerly enslaved Africans, denied land and resources, were left to scrape by through wage tenancy, Metayer (sharecropping), or migratory labor in salt ponds, fisheries, and sugar fields.

25 The Apprenticeship System (1834–1838) was a British colonial labor system that delayed full emancipation by requiring formerly enslaved people to work as "apprentices" for their former masters under harsh conditions.

Parallel Chains

Though oceans apart, the Carolinas and Caribbean shared one truth: **freedom was sabotaged by design.** Both sharecropping and indenture ensured that wealth flowed upward while those at the bottom remained voiceless, landless, and powerless. These systems reproduced slavery's essence: control over bodies, denial of autonomy, and perpetuation of racial hierarchies only now under the veneer of contracts and "free labor."

Where once the lash had enforced obedience, now the law and ledger did. A missed quota or a debt slip replaced the overseer's whip. Still, the outcome was the same: generations locked into cycles of grinding labor, denied the ownership and prosperity that true emancipation required.

Toward Reclamation

In dissecting these traps, we expose their deliberate design: they were not failures of policy but **instruments of empire,** ensuring Black freedom remained a shadow rather than a reality. To reclaim time, land, and vision, we must recognize these continuities and confront the unbroken chains of economic exploitation that stretch from Carolina cotton fields to Caribbean cane brakes. Only then can the descendants of those trapped in these systems build what was denied ownership, sovereignty, and rest.

In the Caribbean, emancipation replaced slavery's name, not its structure. Apprenticeship enforced unpaid labor, while indentured servitude sustained plantation economies by denying land and autonomy to the freed. As in the Carolinas, contracts replaced chains, but the outcome remained the same labor extracted without ownership, freedom constrained by debt and law, and generations bound to a life of "can't see to can't see."

How Sharecropping Mirrored Slavery in America

Sharecropping, the dominant labor system in the post-Civil War South, did not abolish slavery when it rebranded it. In the Carolinas and across the South, the promise of emancipation collapsed into a system that trapped Black families in perpetual debt and dependency, binding them to the very same plantations where they or their parents had once been enslaved. By the 1880s, over 80% of Black farmers in the Carolinas were sharecroppers, their "freedom" reduced to contracts designed to mimic bondage.

The Mechanics of Exploitation

In theory, sharecropping offered freed people the use of land in exchange for a portion of the harvest. In practice, landowners set the rules: families received half or often less of the crop's value after deductions for seed, fertilizer, tools, and food, all supplied by the landowner at inflated prices.

The **crop lien system** guaranteed that debts exceeded earnings year after year. Interest rates soared as high as 50%, ensuring that the little profit made was quickly absorbed by the ledgers controlled by white landlords.

South Carolina's low country tells the story in sharper relief. On Hilton Head and Beaufort islands, Gullah-Geechee families who once envisioned independence on confiscated rice lands were forced back under white absentee owners. They grew rice not for themselves, but for creditors, whose names were tied to debts that kept them bound like serfs. In North Carolina's Piedmont, cotton sharecroppers endured the same fate every boll weighed down by hidden costs that transformed labor into chains.

Law and Violence as Tools of Control

The system was upheld not only by contracts but by coercion. **Black Codes and vagrancy laws** criminalized unemployment, allowing sheriffs to arrest landless freedmen and lease them to white farmers in "slavery by another name." Violence reinforced the trap: landlords threatened eviction, while groups like the **Ku Klux Klan and Red Shirts** unleashed terror lynchings, night raids, and beatings to silence resistance. In 1876, South Carolina's Hamburg Massacre sent a chilling message: Black autonomy would be crushed at gunpoint.

Families Ensnared

Entire households bore the burden. Men, women, and even children as young as six labored in the fields from "can't see to can't see." Education was a dream deferred; when harvest called, schools emptied. Just as under slavery, white supremacy dictated Black family life, not only by stealing labor but by robbing children of futures beyond the hoe and plow.

Economic and Generational Consequences

By 1900, Black land ownership in the Carolinas had declined to below 20%, a devastating reversal from the hopes of independence during the Reconstruction era. Sharecropping ensured that wealth never accumulated in Black hands, fueling the **Great Migration** as thousands fled northward seeking factory work and safety from racial terror. But even migration bore scars: the wealth gap entrenched by sharecropping remains visible today, with Black households holding just 15% of the wealth of white households nationwide.

A Mirror of Slavery

Sharecropping was not an accidental system of poverty; it was slavery reimagined. Where the lash once drove labor, the ledger now did. Where overseers once cracked whips, landlords manipulated debts. Its purpose was not only economic exploitation but also the preservation of racial dominance. For Black Carolinians, emancipation had not opened the door to freedom it had swung them into another cage, proving that chains can be made of numbers as surely as iron.

The economic damage of this system did not end with the contracts that created it. Land loss translated into lost wealth, lost security, and lost generational momentum effects that compound across time. Sharecropping did not merely exploit labor in the present; it engineered inequality into the future, ensuring that freedom without ownership would echo as poverty, displacement, and disparity long after the fields fell silent.

Caribbean Indenture Systems and Generational Poverty

In the Caribbean, the promise of emancipation curdled into betrayal through systems of apprenticeship and indenture structures that stripped liberty of substance and ensured that poverty, not freedom, was inherited. Where American sharecropping bound Black families to cotton and rice fields, Caribbean freed people were shackled to salt pans, cane rows, and colonial overseers under new names but old chains.

Apprenticeship: Slavery in Disguise

When Britain abolished slavery in 1834, emancipation arrived with strings attached. Instead of freedom, ex-slaves entered a four-to-six-year "apprenticeship" scheme that demanded up to 45 hours of unpaid weekly labor for their former masters. Refusal meant vagrancy charges, imprisonment, or flogging. In the Bahamas, more than 10,000 newly freed Africans were compelled to work in cotton fields, salt raking, and sponging under conditions nearly indistinguishable from bondage. Their meager allowances for food and housing were deducted from wages, leaving them with nothing, a mirror of the debt penalty that sharecropping imposed in the Carolinas. Resistance was constant: from the **1830s Pompey Rebellion on Exuma** to smaller work stoppages, freed people protested a "freedom" that offered only new names for old servitude.

Indenture: Importing New Chains

Figure 29 Indian Arrival Month in Guyana, Trinidad, and Jamaica

Once the apprenticeship ended in 1838, planters turned to imported labor. Between 1838 and 1917, more than **500,000 Indians, along with thousands of Chinese and Portuguese workers,** were shipped into colonies such as Trinidad, Guyana, and Jamaica under the banner of indenture. Contracts spanned five to ten years, binding workers to plantations with starvation wages, corporal punishment for "laziness," and restrictions on movement. In reality, indenture was another form of coerced labor designed to stabilize the sugar economy and suppress wages.

In Jamaica and Trinidad, freed Blacks often refused to return to the cane fields under exploitative pay. Planters imported indentured Indians as "coolie labor" to fill the void, intentionally depressing local wages and pitting marginalized groups against one another. This divide-and-rule tactic ensured that Black workers, already landless, were forced into the lowest tiers of labor, sponging, dock work, or migration to neighboring islands, instead of building stable, independent livelihoods.

The results were devastating. In the Bahamas, Crown lands remained in the hands of the elite, preventing freed people from securing economic independence. In Jamaica, the suppression of the **1865 Morant Bay Rebellion,** where land-starved peasants demanded plots, highlighted the fact that emancipation without land meant continued dependency.

Generational Consequences

In Haiti, the debt to France compounded these failures, draining resources that might have been used to build a peasant economy. Across the region, the cycle was the same: labor was extracted, wealth was exported, and freedom was denied.

The indenture formally ended in the early 20th century, but its legacy endured. By importing new labor while denying freed Blacks the land and tools for self-sufficiency, colonial powers entrenched poverty across the Caribbean. Just as sharecropping kept Carolinians "from can't see to can't see," Caribbean apprenticeship and indenture kept entire islands working without reward, ensuring that generations inherited exhaustion instead of equity.

After apprenticeship ended in 1838, Caribbean planters replaced enslaved labor with indentured workers. Between 1838 and 1917, hundreds of thousands of Indians along with Chinese and Portuguese laborers,were imported into colonies such as Trinidad, Guyana, and Jamaica under restrictive contracts. Though labeled free labor, indenture imposed long terms, low wages, limited movement, and harsh punishment, preserving plantation economies while suppressing worker power.

This system was deliberately used to undermine emancipated Black populations. In colonies where freed people resisted returning to exploitative plantation work, planters imported indentured labor to depress wages and divide the working class. Denied land and resources, Black workers were pushed into marginal labor or migration, while colonial elites maintained control through racial stratification and economic exclusion.

Generational Poverty and Colonial Policies of Control

Generational Poverty Across the Caribbean

Emancipation without land was emancipation without a future. In Haiti, independence in 1804 promised liberation, but the crushing 1825 French indemnity of 150 million francs starved the new nation of infrastructure and growth. Estates fractured into smallholdings, but by the 20th century, over **80% of Haitians remained rural and impoverished,** vulnerable to hurricanes and political instability.

In Jamaica, the **1865 Morant Bay Rebellion** exposed the depth of land hunger. Black peasants, facing famine and unemployment, demanded access to land; the British response was brutal hundreds executed, villages burned, and self-governance revoked. Instead of redistribution, repression preserved elite control, cementing cycles of lack.

The end of indenture in the early 20th century brought uneven outcomes. **Indian communities,** though themselves exploited, leveraged small savings and networks to build entrepreneurial footholds. In contrast, most Black populations remained landless, laboring on sugar estates, in dockyards, or in the tourism industry. By mid-century, **poverty rates exceeded 50%** in many islands, proving that slavery's shadow was not erased but institutionalized into generational inheritance. Children grew up with limited education, poor health access, and unstable work, echoing slavery's family disruptions while fueling ethnic tensions that divided laborers against one another.

Colonial Policies Designed to Withhold Power

Caribbean poverty was not an accident, it was engineered. **Britain's Emancipation Act of 1833** compensated slaveholders with £20 million (≈£17 billion today) but gave nothing to the enslaved blacks. Instead, the Crown funded the mass importation of indentured workers, ensuring freed Africans remained cheap, expendable labor.

Laws reinforced this subjugation. In Jamaica and the Bahamas, **"Master and Servant"** statutes criminalized contract breaches, allowing planters-turned-magistrates to jail "idle" workers. Crown land remained locked in elite hands, and taxes on small plots forced Black peasants into wage labor. France mirrored this strategy: Haiti was drained by indemnity payments, while Martinique and Guadeloupe preserved sugar monopolies with imported indentured labor.

The United States extended this model of exploitation beyond its own borders. During its 1915–1934 occupation of Haiti, U.S. forces seized control of customs revenues, diverting them to repay foreign creditors while starving the country of funds needed for schools, infrastructure, and local industry. Forced labor policies were reinstated, and political power was centralized to protect foreign interests. Across the wider Caribbean, colonial and later neocolonial systems reinforced one another, denying land, restricting sovereignty, and keeping Black populations economically dependent and politically weakened, even as formal empire claimed to be ending.

Sustaining Hierarchies Through Policy and Design

These systems were not accidental outcomes of emancipation they were blueprints for control. Colonial and Southern elites deliberately **restricted education,** tying literacy to subordination. They linked **voting rights to property,** ensuring that the very populations denied land ownership could never access political power. When resistance rose, as in Jamaica's 1865 Morant Bay Rebellion, it was met with military slaughter, martial law, and renewed repression.

Environmental legacies compounded bondage. Monocultures of sugar, cotton, and rice exploited under slavery left soils depleted, making independence impossible without resources or redistribution. Yet aid, technology, and land grants were withheld, guaranteeing dependence. Today, this history persists in debt traps: Caribbean nations still owe billions to former colonizers and international banks, their revenues mortgaged much like those of freedmen under sharecropping.

Breaking the Design

Sharecropping's debts, indenture's contracts, and colonial statutes were not the "natural evolution" of post-slavery economies; they were **structures of sabotage,** designed to keep Black communities laboring in the shadows of "can't see to can't see."

Yet even in that darkness, resistance never died. These betrayals now fuel resolve: to reclaim land, build businesses, and tell our own stories. The fight is no longer for survival alone but for sovereignty where our children inherit vision, not chains, and walk in fields they finally own.

What made these systems especially effective was how quietly they operated. Power was not only enforced through violence but embedded into bureaucracy licenses, permits, taxes, property surveys, and legal delays that appeared neutral while functioning as barriers. Freedom was surrounded by paperwork that the newly emancipated were never equipped or allowed to navigate. Control no longer needed spectacle; it lived in offices, registries, and courts where exclusion was rendered administrative rather than overt.

This bureaucratic grip shaped everyday life. Economic decisions where one could live, farm, vote, borrow, or trade were predetermined by structures that rewarded proximity to whiteness and punished independence. Mobility became conditional, opportunity selective, and advancement rare. Over time, this manufactured scarcity trained generations to adapt rather than challenge, to survive within constraints rather than demand their removal. Dependence was not a failure of ambition but the expected outcome of the design.

As formal empire receded, these arrangements did not disappear; they localized. Political elites inherited colonial frameworks and often governed through them, maintaining land concentration and external dependency while promising reform. International lenders replaced imperial treasuries, development loans replaced indemnities, and austerity replaced whips. The language softened, but the hierarchy endured extraction upward, discipline downward.

Understanding this continuity clarifies the task ahead. The struggle is not against history but against its unfinished architecture. True emancipation requires dismantling systems that ration power while calling it freedom. It demands restructuring ownership, access, and decision-making so that labor no longer feeds distant centers while communities remain depleted. Only then can movement replace stagnation, and freedom finally mean more than endurance.

Chapter 7

MIGRANTS WITH THE SAME BURDEN

Waves of migration carried the weary across borders, but the burden clung like a shadow stitched into their skin. From the dusty roads of the Carolinas to the crowded docks of Kingston and Nassau, Black folk moved with hope in their hearts and chains still on their backs.

In the United States, the Great Migration saw Gullah-Geechee kin ride rails northward, leaving rice swamps for Harlem streets, cotton fields for Chicago stockyards, seeking wages, dignity, and escape from lynch mobs. Yet the refrain of "from can't see to can't see" echoed still, now in factory night shifts, steel mills, and domestic labor that devoured body and soul.

Across the Atlantic, Caribbean families boarded ships bound for Britain, Canada, and the United States. Jamaicans disembarked in London to work the buses and railways; Bahamians swept into Miami's hotels and New York's kitchens; Barbadians bent their backs on British construction sites.

The seas had carried them away from plantations, but into the arms of new overseers' employers who paid pennies, landlords who barred doors, governments that stamped "immigrant" where "citizen" should have been.

Migration became survival, not salvation. It relocated the grind rather than removed it. Families were split; cultures diluted; accents mocked in schools and jobs. Yet resilience traveled too: Gullah songs blended with Harlem jazz; Junkanoo drums echoed in the streets of London; Bahamian straw work adorned the markets of New York. These carried memory and defiance, reminding each generation that the burden was shared, and so was the strength.

This diaspora was not an escape but an adaptation. By tracing these paths, we see the unbroken thread: migration as movement without freedom, labor without ownership. The lesson is clear salvation cannot be found in flight alone. It demands roots, land, and legacy built where we stand, so the next generation walks unburdened.

Great Migration (U.S.) and Caribbean Diaspora Labor

The Great Migration in the United States and the Caribbean diaspora were twin exoduses, propelled by Jim Crow terror, economic despair, and colonial neglect. From Carolina cotton fields to Bahamian salt pans, Black communities fled the old order, only to meet new forms of labor extraction that kept freedom incomplete.

In the U.S., the Great Migration unfolded in two vast waves (1910–1940 and 1940–1970), drawing over six million African Americans from the rural South into Northern cities. From the Carolinas, hundreds of thousands left boll weevil infestations destroyed cotton, sharecropping debts strangled families, and lynch mobs over 500 recorded in the Carolinas between

1882 and 1968 made survival precarious. World Wars opened industrial doors: factories, shipyards, and auto plants recruited Southern migrants with promises of steady pay. But the rhythm of exploitation persisted. Assembly lines became new plantations, and while some migrants built middle-class footholds, many found themselves in urban poverty, battling overcrowded housing, discrimination, and higher mortality rates than the white working class.

Across the sea, the Caribbean diaspora mirrored this flight. Following World War II, colonial economies struggled under the pressures of decolonization and global economic downturns, prompting massive migrations to the United States, Canada, and the United Kingdom. Britain's 1948 Nationality Act offered Commonwealth citizens the right to settle, giving rise to the Windrush generation: over 800,000 migrants by 1971, comprising many Jamaicans, Barbadians, and Bahamians, who filled buses, hospitals, and factories. Like their U.S. kin, they met racism at every turn "No Blacks, No Irish, No Dogs" signs in London echoed Jim Crow restrictions in the American South.

Both migrations reshaped the Black Atlantic. They built churches, unions, and cultural movements, but also transplanted plantation hierarchies into cities, where "from can't see to can't see" meant night shifts and double jobs instead of cane fields and cotton rows. What united them was the search for dignity and the bitter discovery that mobility alone could not undo bondage without ownership, equity, and land.

The Great Migration and the Caribbean diaspora were parallel flights from racial terror and economic exclusion, carrying Black communities from Southern fields and Caribbean plantations into Northern cities and imperial centers. Yet migration did not end exploitation it relocated it. Factories, shipyards, and service work replaced cotton and cane, but long hours, discrimination, and insecurity endured. Across the Black Atlantic, survived the journey, revealing that movement without ownership or equity could not complete the promise of freedom.

Intra-Caribbean and Transnational Labor Migrations

In the United States, the 20th century saw new Caribbean tides join the Great Migration's current. Haitians fled the iron grip of the Duvalier dictatorships from the 1950s through the 1980s, seeking asylum in Miami, New York, and beyond. Bahamians and Jamaicans crossed borders through U.S. H-2 farm programs, cutting cane and picking crops in the Carolinas and Florida, seasonal labor that echoed their ancestors' Loyalist-era transplantations.

Within the Caribbean itself, migration followed the same exploitative pattern. Haitians crossed into the Dominican Republic or the Bahamas for back-breaking cane work, often facing deportation, abuse, and statelessness. Labor demand transformed Black mobility into a commodified circulation, rather than liberation.

This movement carried a high cost: brain drain. By the late 20th century, more than 60% of tertiary-educated Caribbeans had emigrated, hollowing out the professional classes in Jamaica, Haiti, and Guyana. Remittances, now exceeding $30 billion annually, have become lifelines for families left behind, but they cannot replace the wealth stolen through centuries of denied ownership.

These streams converged abroad. In Harlem, Brooklyn, and Miami, Carolina descendants rubbed shoulders with new arrivals from Kingston, Nassau, and Port-au-Prince. They shared pews in Black churches, crowded into the same neighborhoods, and filled the same undervalued jobs, nursing, domestic work, factory shifts. Though their accents differed, their labor echoed the same refrain: "from can't see to can't see," survival without sovereignty, toil without inheritance.

Low-Paying Domestic and Service Work in Foreign Lands

Migration did not free Black workers from bondage; it repositioned them at the bottom of foreign economies, where domestic and service labor became the default. These jobs, cooking, cleaning, caretaking, carrying bags, were the modern plantations of the U.S. and UK, fueled by Black hands yet invisible in the wealth they sustained.

In the United States, migrants from the Carolinas' Great Migration streamed into segregated cities only to find themselves funneled into service roles. Black women became domestics in white households, maids, cooks, and nannies, while men worked as porters, janitors, and drivers, earning pennies on the dollar compared to white workers. Even in unions, they were often excluded or pushed to the lowest ranks, their sweat enriching industries that denied them equity.

Caribbean arrivals mirrored this pattern. Bahamians and Jamaicans in Florida's fields or New York's boroughs took jobs as farm laborers, hotel staff, or nursing aides. Bound by exploitative visa programs like H-2A, many endured sub-minimum wages, wage theft, and unsafe conditions, silenced by employer-tied immigration status. Haitians who fled by boat in the 1980s found themselves detained, deported, or trapped in sweatshops and caregiving roles, exposed to harassment and trafficking, with little recourse.

Systemic exploitation made these conditions possible. Until the 1970s, U.S. minimum wage laws excluded domestic workers entirely, legalizing unpaid overtime and abuse. Black women reported wage theft and sexual harassment at double the rates of their white counterparts.

This was not freedom, it was continuity. The broom replaced the hoe, the hotel replaced the plantation, but the rhythm remained the same: "from can't see to can't see." Migration became less about mobility and more about maintaining global hierarchies where Black labor fueled prosperity, but Black communities remained in poverty.

Service Work and Exploitation in the UK

For Caribbean migrants in the UK, the promise of opportunity quickly soured into the reality of exploitation. Windrush-era Jamaicans and Bahamians, recruited to rebuild Britain's postwar economy, filled critical roles in the NHS and London Transport, working long hours for meager wages. Instead of gratitude, they found "No Blacks" signs on boarding houses, slum accommodations, and systemic hostility that marked them as outsiders in the very nation they had been called to serve.

Domestic work became another trap. Haitian and Jamaican women cleaned homes, cared for children, and tended to the elderly, but endured racial slurs, withheld pay, and constant vulnerability tied to their immigration status. Their visas often bound them to single employers, creating a modern indenture were leaving meant deportation.

Policies only deepened the chains. Britain's "hostile environment" of the 2010s deported even long-term residents who had arrived legally decades earlier. Recruitment fees in home countries forced workers into debt bondage before they even boarded the ship or plane. Service industries, such as hotels, restaurants, and cleaning agencies, absorbed migrants into precarious, low-paying jobs with limited opportunities for advancement.

The COVID-19 pandemic stripped away any illusions. Black workers, disproportionately concentrated in care work and other essential but undervalued jobs, faced higher death rates, the result of overexposure, poor protections, and systemic neglect.

These roles were not ladders upward; they were pits. Meant scrubbing floors and changing sheets by day and night, laboring without ownership of time, home, or future. Britain, like America, rebranded the plantation, keeping Caribbean migrants at the bottom, holding up an empire that refused to see them as equals.

For Caribbean migrants in the UK, postwar recruitment quickly gave way to exploitation. Windrush-era Jamaicans and Bahamians were funneled into essential roles in the NHS, transport, and municipal services, working long hours for low pay while facing housing discrimination and open racial hostility. They were summoned to rebuild Britain, yet treated as disposable outsiders within the very system they sustained.

Domestic and care work deepened this vulnerability. Caribbean women, and later Haitian migrants, labored as cleaners, caregivers, and nannies under conditions that echoed indenture, tied to single employers, exposed to abuse, and threatened with deportation if they resisted. Immigration policies and recruitment fees compounded this precarity, pushing workers into debt before arrival and locking them into service industries with little chance of advancement.

The pandemic exposed the full cost of this arrangement. Black migrants, overrepresented in essential care and service roles, faced disproportionate illness and death amid poor protections and systemic neglect. These jobs were never pathways to security; they were mechanisms of containment. In Britain, as in America, "from can't see to can't see" simply changed form,long shifts replacing plantation rows,revealing how empire endured by rebranding exploitation while denying equality, rest, and ownership.

Chapter 8

THE POOR WHO CAN'T STOP WORKING

The cotton rows have vanished, but the grind remains relentless, bone-deep, and inherited from centuries of labor without rest. Today, the fields have gone digital, but the exhaustion is still analog: raw, endless, and designed to wring every ounce of life from the poor. Black folk hustle through gig apps[26], night shifts, and side hustles, trading plantation whips for algorithm bosses, overseers for app notifications.

"From can't see to can't see" has simply shifted form. Where once dawn meant the rice swamp and dusk meant the cane field, now it means scrolling for rides at sunrise and dropping off packages by moonlight. Rest is no longer stolen it is marketed as indulgence. Burnout has become a badge of honor, even as corporations quietly siphon billions from those who can't afford to pause.

26 Gig apps (short for "gig economy apps") are mobile platforms that connect independent workers (often called "gig workers") with short-term, flexible jobs or tasks.

The trap is deliberate. Sharecropping's debts morphed into payday loans and credit traps; apprenticeship contracts reappeared in zero-hour jobs and gig precarity. The same structural lack, no land, no capital, no cushion keeps Black workers moving endlessly, running on treadmills disguised as opportunities.

In Charleston warehouses or Nassau's tourist corridors, Kingston's call centers or Port-au-Prince's street corners, the story repeats: the poor can't stop working. Not because they lack willpower, but because the system was engineered to deny them rest, stability, and ownership. This chapter pulls back the curtain on the "modern grind," revealing that what we call progress is often nothing more than ancient chains reforged proof that emancipation without equity is just another word for exhaustion.

Gig Economy, Shift Work, and Multiple Job Survival

The gig economy and shift work have become lifelines lined with thorns modern survival strategies that echo the endless toil of plantation days, only now mediated by apps and algorithms instead of overseers. Freedom has been rebranded as "flexibility," but for millions of Black workers, flexibility means instability, precarity, and exhaustion.

In the United States, over 70 million people now rely on gig work (as of 2025), projected to surpass 86 million by 2027. Platforms like Uber, DoorDash, and TaskRabbit dominate, yet behind the glossy promise of "being your own boss" lies a grind of unpredictable earnings, no benefits, and hidden costs. Black workers are disproportionately caught in this net: 27% of Black adults engage in gig work, compared to lower rates among whites, often stacking it on top of low-wage primary jobs to keep the lights on.

The Carolinas tell the story vividly. Once rice and cotton country, they are now dotted with Amazon warehouses and rideshare pickups new fields where Black labor still fuels profits without ownership. Warehouse shifts mean nights without sleep, rideshare gigs consume car maintenance like crop liens consume harvests, and "independent contractor" status denies access to healthcare, sick leave, or pensions. It is sharecropping with an app.

Shift work compounds the squeeze. Black workers make up 25% of warehouse jobs while only 12% of the workforce, overrepresented in roles with irregular schedules that fracture family life and corrode health. Healthcare aides, janitors, drivers these "essential" roles carry the same paradox as slavery once did: the system cannot function without Black labor, yet it refuses to value it.

The survival strategy has become juggling. As of mid-2025, 8.9 million Americans 5.3% of all workers hold multiple jobs, the highest in decades. Young adults and women lead the way, clocking 60+ hours a week across shifts and side hustles, trading rest for rent, stability for survival. The toll is visible in chronic fatigue, rising hypertension, and fractured communities where parents tuck children into bed between gigs.

What looks like hustle culture is in truth the latest mask of bondage. "From can't see to can't see" has not vanished it has simply migrated into digital platforms, warehouse floors, and shift rotations. The plantation never ended; it just rebranded with a login screen.

Gig Economy, Shift Work, and Multiple Job Survival

The gig economy and shift work have become lifelines lined with thorns modern survival strategies that echo the endless toil of plantation days, only now mediated by apps and algorithms instead of overseers. Freedom has been rebranded as "flexibility," but for millions of Black workers, flexibility means instability, precarity, and exhaustion.

In the United States, over 70 million people now rely on gig work (as of 2025), projected to surpass 86 million by 2027. Platforms like Uber, DoorDash, and TaskRabbit dominate, yet behind the glossy promise of "being your own boss" lies a grind of unpredictable earnings, no benefits, and hidden costs. Black workers are disproportionately caught in this net: 27% of Black adults engage in gig work, compared to lower rates among whites, often stacking it on top of low-wage primary jobs to keep the lights on.

The Carolinas show this vividly. Once rice and cotton country, they are now dotted with Amazon warehouses and rideshare pickups new fields where Black labor still fuels profits without ownership. Warehouse shifts mean nights without sleep, rideshare gigs consume car maintenance like crop liens consume harvests, and "independent contractor" status denies access to healthcare, sick leave, or pensions. It is sharecropping with an app.

Shift work compounds the squeeze. Black workers make up 25% of warehouse jobs while only 12% of the workforce, overrepresented in roles with irregular schedules that fracture family life and corrode health. Healthcare aides, janitors, drivers these "essential" roles carry the same paradox as slavery once did: the system cannot function without Black labor, yet it refuses to value it.

The survival strategy has become juggling. As of mid-2025, 8.9 million Americans 5.3% of all workers hold multiple jobs, the highest in decades. Young adults and women lead the way, clocking 60+ hours a week across shifts and side hustles, trading rest for rent, stability for survival.

Across the Caribbean, the patterns echo. Gig and shift work is prevalent in tourism, hospitality, and informal economies. In Nassau or Kingston, hotel night shifts churn on poverty wages even as tourists pour in. App-based ride-hailing and freelance platforms are growing in Jamaica and the Bahamas, while in Haiti, moto-taxis and street vending serve as unregulated gig work, with insecurity and power outages turning survival into a hazard. For many, one job is never enough: Jamaicans often hold formal roles by day and gig by night, while workers in Colombia's Caribbean coast average just $560/month well below living costs.

Remittances patch the gaps but also underscore dependence. Carolinas-based relatives send money home, sometimes financing gig startups, yet the grind persists, rooted in the same structural lack. Regional growth in 2025 lags at 2.3%, leaving few formal jobs and pushing entire populations into precarious labor.

What looks like hustle culture is, in truth, the latest mask of bondage. "From can't see to can't see" has not vanished it has simply migrated into digital platforms, hotel shifts, and street stalls. The plantation never ended; it just rebranded with apps, uniforms, and tourist tips.

The gig economy, shift work, and multiple-job survival represent the latest rebranding of extraction. Marketed as flexibility, these systems deliver instability unpredictable wages, no benefits, and endless hours disproportionately borne by Black workers. From Amazon warehouses and rideshare pickups in the Carolinas to hotel night shifts, tourism labor, and informal gig work across the Caribbean, labor fuels profit without ownership or security. Many workers juggle two or three jobs, trading rest for rent and health for survival, while remittances merely patch gaps created by structural deprivation. What passes as hustle culture is, in truth, digital sharecropping: migrated into apps, shift rotations, and service economies. The plantation did not disappear it learned how to log in.

Wage Stagnation vs. Cost of Living

Wages have flatlined while living costs soar, creating a chasm that swallows Black households in the Carolinas and Caribbean. Historical inequities amplify the squeeze, forcing endless labor just to stay afloat.

In the United States, real wages have stagnated for over 15 years. Average hourly earnings rise only 3.2% annually amid inflation, but for low-wage Black workers, gains vanish under a 20% racial pay gap. By 2025, 73% of workers report struggling with wages versus costs, with housing, food, and healthcare costs inflating by 4–7% yearly. In the Carolinas, the median Black household income hovers around $45,000 far below the $ 60,000 or more needed in urban areas like Charlotte or Charleston. Rents have risen 10% since 2023, pushing families into multiple jobs. This isn't individual failure it's policy neglect: the federal minimum wage has been frozen at $7.25 since 2009, while inflation-adjusted needs top $10, hitting service-heavy Black communities hardest.

Caribbean parallels are just as dire. In Jamaica, 91% of roles pay below regional averages, with minimum wage hikes offset by surges of 20% or more in food and energy costs. In the Bahamas and Haiti, import dependence makes groceries 50% more expensive than the U.S. average, while wages stagnate at $200–$400/month for many, far below the survival threshold. Regional growth at 2.3% (2025) offers no relief, as debt burdens from colonial indemnities siphon funds that could lift wages. Diaspora remittances $30 billion annually patch holes but expose dependence, as workers abroad send home income from their own low-wage gigs.

This mismatch isn't a market hiccup; it is a continuation of a systemic design flaw. From denied reparations to land theft, Black communities were stripped of wealth cushions. Today, every price hike cuts deeper because there is no inherited land, no accumulated capital, no safety net. The result is familiar: Black families working harder for less, their sweat enriching others while their own households remain one bill away from crisis.

Like the cane fields and cotton rows, the modern wage economy keeps us grinding "from can't see to can't see" not because we are unwilling, but because the system was never built for us to rest.

The Glorification of Overwork, and Who Profits from It

Hustle culture cloaks exploitation in empowerment, glorifying overwork as virtue while masking its toll on Black communities' burnout, health crises, family strain all while corporations extract billions from cheap, disposable labor.

In Black spaces, hustle has always been a survival strategy, born from wage gaps, exclusion, and historical necessity. But today it is rebranded and monetized social media mantras like "sleep when you're dead" glamorize 60-hour weeks, even as Black workers earn 20% less than their white peers. What is often framed as ambition can produce only exhaustion. The results are measurable: disproportionate rates of hypertension, diabetes, and stress disorders in Black communities' modern echoes of slavery's relentless toll on the body.

In the Carolinas and Caribbean diaspora, the cycle intensifies. A Bahamian hotel worker might clock 16-hour shifts during peak tourist season serving cocktails by day, cleaning rooms by night yet still return home to unpaid debts and soaring grocery prices. Meanwhile, a North Carolina warehouse worker for Amazon may grind overnight shifts, sprinting miles across concrete floors to meet impossible quotas, only to face injuries, surveillance, and stagnant wages. Both are told they are "lucky" to have work. Both are praised as "hardworking." And both collapse into bed, too tired to build wealth, too drained to dream.

Hustle is sold as resilience but resilience without rest is just repackaged bondage. This culture profits the few and drains the many. Where enslavers once extracted sugar and cotton, today corporations extract time, health, and dignity, feeding on the endless motion of the poor. The plantation whip has been replaced with motivational slogans, but the rhythm is the same: "from can't see to can't see," laboring without ownership while someone else reaps the wealth.

Who Profits from the Grind?

The winners are not the workers they are the platforms and corporations that disguise exploitation as opportunity. Gig giants like Uber and DoorDash, valued at hundreds of billions of dollars, take 20–30% cuts from rides and meals while classifying drivers as "contractors" and stripping them of benefits. Amazon and Walmart, empire builders of warehouse shifts and retail gigs, post record profits while injuries, exhaustion, and low wages pile up among their Black labor force. By 2025, the global gig economy swelled past $600 billion, but the wealth flowed upward into executive bonuses and shareholder dividends.

The Caribbean faces its mirror image. Tourism giants in Nassau, Montego Bay, and Port of Spain extract relentless labor from housekeepers, cooks, and bellmen, while profits are sent overseas to foreign corporate headquarters. A Bahamian worker may toil double shifts at a luxury resort yet remain unable to afford basic groceries, which are priced higher than in U.S. cities. The hustle is marketed as resilience, but it is a form of structured dependency: locals work hard so that outsiders can reap the benefits.

The myth of hustle sustains inequality across borders. Black workers from Charleston to Kingston are praised as "hardworking," but what is really being celebrated is their disposability the ease with which their labor can be wrung dry and replaced. The glorification of overwork isn't about empowerment; it's about profit.

But resistance is stirring. A growing call to reject hustle culture what some frame as embracing a more balanced approach prioritizes health, balance, and ownership over the relentless grind. The poor who can't stop working embody ancient chains in modern disguise. Yet by exposing who profits, we also uncover who must reclaim power: the workers whose time, bodies, and futures have always been the real wealth. True freedom means refusing to let labor be the only inheritance, demanding ownership, rest, and dignity across the sea and across generations.

The primary beneficiaries of the grind are not the workers but the corporations that monetize precarity. Gig platforms extract substantial cuts from every transaction while avoiding responsibility for wages, healthcare, or job security, and logistics and retail giants report record profits built on warehouse labor that is underpaid and injury-prone. As the global gig economy expands, wealth concentrates at the top channeled into executive compensation and shareholder returns while the labor force absorbs the risk and exhaustion.

Across the Caribbean, the pattern repeats under a different banner. Tourism economies in Nassau, Montego Bay, and Port of Spain depend on long hours from hotel and service workers whose wages rarely cover the cost of living. Profits are exported to foreign owners, while locals are praised for "resilience" and left managing scarcity. What appears as opportunity is, in practice, a system that converts hard work into dependency rather than advancement.

The celebration of hustle sustains this imbalance. Black workers from the Caribbean are lauded for endurance, even as that endurance is exploited and easily replaced. Yet awareness is shifting. Calls to reject hustle culture and prioritize health, ownership, and time signal a deeper challenge to the grind itself. Exposing who profits clarifies the next step: reclaiming labor's value so that work no longer consumes life, and freedom is measured not by endurance, but by dignity, rest, and shared prosperity.

PART THREE

MODERN GRIND, ANCIENT CHAINS

Chapter 9

ESSENTIAL AND EXPENDABLE

The COVID-19 pandemic did not invent inequality, it magnified it, casting a spotlight on the fractures that had long been ignored. When the world shut down in 2020, the term "essential worker" was coined as if it were an honor. Yet in the Carolinas' warehouses, Nassau's resorts, Kingston's markets, and Port-au-Prince's streets, it quickly became clear: essential meant expendable.

Black and brown bodies, already bound by centuries of denied wealth and health, became the backbone that kept economies alive while bearing the greatest risk of death. Nurses without proper PPE, grocery clerks facing unmasked crowds, farmhands laboring shoulder-to-shoulder in fields, delivery drivers hustling through lockdowns all were praised in speeches but abandoned in practice. Praise was free; protection was scarce.

The irony was cruel. Those most necessary to survival feeding, healing, transporting were the least shielded, the least paid, the least insured. In the U.S., Black people were nearly twice as likely to die of COVID-19 as whites, a reflection of overcrowded housing, frontline exposure, and pre-existing conditions rooted in systemic neglect. In the Caribbean, the collapse of tourism led to layoffs for thousands, forcing many into informal hustle that exposed them to further risks, while governments touted their resilience.

The pandemic rebranded an old reality: from slavery's fields to sharecropping's debts, from migration's low-wage traps to the gig economy's shifts, Black labor has always been "essential" but never secure. COVID simply stripped away the illusion.

To name us essential without granting protection, fair pay, or ownership is exploitation dressed as honor. True recognition requires more than applause at dusk or hashtags at dawn, it demands land, wealth, and safeguards that cannot be rationed or revoked. Until then, "essential" will remain another word for disposable, and the grind from "can't see to can't see" will persist under new masks.

The Pandemic and the Rise of "Essential Worker" Rhetoric

When COVID-19 erupted in early 2020, a new phrase entered the global lexicon: essential worker. Overnight, it became a cultural mantra plastered on banners, hashtags, and government decrees praising frontline laborers as heroes. Yet behind the applause lay a cruel continuity: Black and brown bodies, historically deemed indispensable, were once again declared vital for survival while denied true protection or compensation.

By March 2020, U.S. states such as South Carolina and North Carolina had exempted millions from stay-at-home orders, thereby allowing them to maintain essential food, healthcare, and supply chains. Globally, governments and the World Health Organization amplified the rhetoric.

Campaigns like "clap for carers" in the UK or "heroes work here" signs at U.S. hospitals painted the crisis as a war, with workers framed as soldiers. But soldiers without armor: nurses in Charleston worked double shifts with inadequate PPE, while delivery drivers in Nassau navigated curfews at their own risk.

Caribbean leaders echoed the same script. Bahamian and Jamaican officials hailed tourism and agricultural workers as the backbone of national survival, invoking solidarity in speeches. Haitian authorities called informal vendors and moto drivers "essential" even as outbreaks surged, yet protections never reached the streets. By 2022, as vaccines rolled out and the rhetoric faded, its legacy remained a hollow honorific that increased visibility without empowerment, glorifying sacrifice while withholding safety.

This was not new. The language of indispensability dates to plantation days, when enslaved labor was praised as the "lifeblood" of the empire, and to post-emancipation, when Caribbean sugar workers were deemed vital but left landless. The pandemic merely revived the trope. "Essential" did not mean valued; it meant exposed. It was a linguistic mask for exploitation, keeping economies afloat while the vulnerable bore the brunt.

Black and Brown Workers on the Frontlines Without Protection

Black and brown workers weren't simply labeled essential during COVID-19 they were treated as sacrificial. They bore the heaviest burdens, overrepresented in frontline roles yet under protected, revealing the fault lines where labor, race, and health collide.

In the U.S., Black Americans made up only 12% of the population but 22% of essential workers. Latinos, comprising 18% of the nation, filled 25% of frontline jobs such as warehouses, farms, and transit where remote work was never an option. In the Carolinas, this meant slaughterhouses in South Carolina and tobacco fields in North Carolina became viral hotbeds, where Black and immigrant hands kept production alive while facing death at 2–3 times the rate of whites.

The risks weren't abstract they were amplified by history. Preexisting conditions like hypertension and diabetes, rooted in food deserts and decades of medical neglect, turned infection into fatality. PPE shortages deepened the crisis: by spring 2020, only 38% of Black healthcare workers reported adequate masks, leaving nurses in Charleston and aides in Raleigh hospitals fashioning makeshift gear. Infection rates soared 3–4 times higher for Black and Latino workers because exposure was constant, protection was absent, and choice was nonexistent.

This wasn't heroism, it was coercion dressed in praise. Applause substituted for armor, slogans for safety, leaving Black and brown communities to absorb the virus's brunt. COVID didn't create this inequality; it magnified an old truth: the same bodies once bound to fields "from can't see to can't see" were again tethered to survival shifts, essential to everyone but expendable to the system.

Caribbean and Global Frontlines

In the Caribbean, the pattern was unmissable. Haiti's essential workers mostly informal laborers, overwhelmingly Black endured outbreaks with no PPE, no hospitals equipped to shield them, and no safety nets, cementing racialized health disparities in one of the hemisphere's most underfunded systems. In the Bahamas and Jamaica, where tourism accounts for over half of GDP, Black and brown hotel staff served guests without protections. At the same time, Latino migrant workers in construction and agriculture shouldered added layers of risk and invisibility.

Globally, poverty and discrimination magnify danger. Overcrowded housing left no room for distancing. Telework was a privilege accessible to only 19% of Black workers compared to 38% of Asians forcing Black and brown families into physical jobs with daily exposure. By 2022, U.S. Black mortality from COVID was 2.5 times that of whites, while Caribbean nations recorded spikes tied to tourism reopenings that put profit over protection.

This was not a coincidence, it was continuity. From redlining in the U.S. to land denial in the Caribbean, systemic design funneled Black and brown communities into high-risk, low-protection roles. "Essential" became less a badge of honor than a verdict: indispensable enough to risk, expendable enough to sacrifice.

The Contradiction of Praise Without Pay

Applause echoed from balconies, but pockets stayed empty. The pandemic's greatest hypocrisy was this: showering essential workers with verbal tributes while denying hazard pay, protection, and fair wages. Praise became a substitute for justice, profiting employers while exposing the expendability of Black and brown lives.

Hazard pay was the flashpoint. In 2020, the U.S. HEROES Act promised $13/hour bonuses, but by 2021, most workers had seen nothing. Where pay appeared, it disappeared quickly: in the Carolinas, food workers lost bonuses within months, even as outbreaks spread. Corporations like Amazon and Walmart plastered "heroes work here" across warehouses, then quietly cut hazard pay while recording record-breaking profits. Nurses in Charleston were forced to reuse masks, while sick leave exclusions left many Black workers without income when infected.

The Caribbean chorus was no different. In Nassau's resorts, workers kept hotels afloat without hazard boosts. Jamaican nurses staged protests over unpaid wages and PPE shortages. Haiti's informal economy market vendors, moto drivers labored unprotected, invisible to state relief.

This wasn't oversight, it was design. Low wages subsidize corporate windfalls and national economies. By avoiding raises or permanent protections, U.S. firms alone saved billions while frontline families buried their dead. By 2025, reflections on COVID reveal the bitter irony: essential labor was glorified when convenient, but without sustained pay or protection, the label meant what it always had indispensable yet disposable.

Essential Yet Expendable

The pandemic stripped bare the old chains: Black and brown workers deemed essential, yet treated as expendable, carrying frontline peril without reward. From Carolina clinics to Caribbean counters, labor kept nations alive while lives were left unprotected.

This contradiction demands reckoning. To be "essential" must mean more than slogans it must mean ownership of labor's value, protections enshrined as rights, and pay that honors live rather than exploits them. Anything less repeats history: applause without justice, survival without dignity.

Only by breaking this cycle by naming worth, demanding equity, and reclaiming rest can we see clearly beyond the veil of survival and step into the freedom our ancestors envisioned.

Chapter 10

MODERN LABOR IN THE CARIBBEAN

The sun-kissed shores of the Caribbean hide in a storm of stagnation, where postcard seas mask economies chained to borrowed time and foreign whims. From Nassau's glittering resorts to Bridgtown's restless streets and Port-au-Prince's struggling markets, modern labor echoes the unyielding grind of ancestors now repackaged in uniforms, shift rotations, and gig apps. "From can't see to can't see" endures greeting tourists at dawn, scrubbing hotel floors at dusk, or driving ride-hail cars through sleepless nights.

These islands, once bound by plantations, remain tethered to tourism's fickle tide. Billions flow in through cruise ships, foreign hotels, and remittance economies yet much of that wealth is siphoned abroad, leaving locals struggling to make a living on precarious wages. In Jamaica, hotel staff earn less than living wages despite record tourist arrivals. In the Bahamas, hospitality workers bear double shifts while executives abroad pocket profits. In Haiti, garment factories and informal vendors keep the economy afloat, but foreign debt and disasters magnify precarity. Even new industries, such as call centers in the Dominican Republic and offshore services in Barbados mirror the old pattern: labor is exported, ownership is imported.

Education sparks hope, but without capital to absorb skilled youth, diplomas too often become tickets out, fueling brain drain instead of local transformation. Those who remain face burnout, their ambition dimmed by cycles of low pay and high costs.

This is not progress; it is a polished trap colonial extraction dressed in modern branding. To confront it, we must name the invisible overseers: global capital demanding cheap labor, and local complacency that accepts dependency as destiny. True freedom means seizing ownership of land, industry, and innovation building economies where our sweat enriches our own people, not foreign shareholders.

Tourism Dependency and Foreign-Controlled Economies

Tourism isn't merely an industry in the Caribbean, it is the backbone, propping up economies yet keeping them fragile, dependent, and externally controlled. Across the region, it accounts for over 22% of GDP and employs nearly 2.75 million people, but this lifeblood flows outward. Profits are repatriated to foreign investors while locals absorb the costs in low wages, seasonal instability, and economic vulnerability.

In the Bahamas, tourism accounts for more than 50% of the GDP, with recovery reaching 85–95% of pre-2020 levels by early 2025. Yet the pandemic exposed its fragility: when borders closed, unemployment spiked to 25%, families faced hunger, and entire islands were left adrift.

Jamaica mirrors this dependency: tourism drives 30% of the economy, but U.S. and European chains dominate 70–80% of the high-end resort market, importing food, furniture, and even staff while exporting profits. Local communities are left with unstable gigs that vanish in off-seasons or hurricanes, echoing plantation economies where labor was abundant, but ownership was denied.

Haiti's tourism, contributing less than 5% of GDP, reveals the same trap in its infancy. Foreign investors eye pristine beaches and rich history, yet instability, corruption, and broken infrastructure block self-sustained growth, ensuring reliance on aid rather than equity.

Tourism dependency is not freedom it is a polished form of colonial extraction. Hurricanes, pandemics, and recessions can undo decades of growth overnight, underscoring the fragility of this reliance on it. Until the Caribbean owns its tourism industries, diversifies beyond them, and invests profits into people rather than foreign shareholders, the region will remain chained to a global plantation in paradise's disguise.

Neocolonial Grip: Debt, Dependency, and Climate Fragility

This foreign control is not benign, it is a neocolonial grip, where multinational corporations and foreign governments dictate terms, extracting value while leaving risk behind. The Caribbean's dependence on tourism makes it hostage to outside forces: over 80% of energy imports are fossil fuels, fueling resorts while deepening climate vulnerability in a region already battered by rising seas and stronger hurricanes. Beaches erode to protect foreign investments, while locals bear the brunt of climate chaos.

Debt tightens the chains. Jamaica and the Bahamas owe billions in external loans, with tourism revenues being funneled to creditors instead of being invested in schools, hospitals, or diversification. Regional growth just 2.3% in 2025 barely scratches survival, as debt servicing outweighs development. The result is a cycle: foreign investors profit, while governments mortgage their future to pay yesterday's bills.

"Foreignization" hollows out local economies. Resorts hire expatriate managers, import food instead of buying from local farmers, and shelter profits offshore, dodging taxes. Communities are left grinding "from can't see to can't see" in low-wage service roles, without ownership of the wealth they generate. External shocks magnify the fragility: the 2025 U.S. travel advisories and threatened bans over crime or instability show how swiftly foreign powers can weaken local economies with a single decree.

This is not simply economics it is the modern plantation system, run by corporations instead of colonizers, reinforced by banks instead of chains. True resilience demands rupture: local ownership of tourism, expansion into eco-tourism and community-based enterprises, and bold investments in agriculture, technology, and renewable energy. Only then can the Caribbean transform paradise from an exploited backdrop into a homeland of power, dignity, and sustainability.

This neocolonial grip operates through debt, dependency, and climate exposure, allowing foreign corporations and governments to extract value while leaving Caribbean nations to absorb the risk. Tourism-dominated economies remain hostage to external markets, fossil-fuel dependence, and climate shocks, as revenues are diverted to service foreign debt rather than build local resilience. Profits flow offshore, decision-making stays abroad, and communities are confined to low-wage service work, grinding "from can't see to can't see" without ownership of the wealth they produce. What emerges is a modern plantation system corporate in form, financial in enforcement one that can only be broken through local ownership, economic diversification, and investments that convert survival into sovereignty.

Education Without Opportunity

Education in the Caribbean promises a ladder out of poverty, but too often it ends at a dead end. High literacy rates and near-universal enrollment mask a harsher reality: degrees accumulate while jobs disappear, leaving graduates underemployed, overqualified, or forced to migrate. In Jamaica, youth unemployment hovers around 30%, while in the Bahamas it exceeds 20%, creating a cycle where classrooms brim with potential, but economies cannot absorb it.

This contradiction has roots in colonial systems designed to produce clerks and compliant workers rather than innovators or landowners. The legacy persists: even as students excel, economies dependent on tourism and foreign capital offer little beyond low-wage service jobs. Education becomes a ticket abroad rather than a tool for transformation at home, fueling the brain drain, where over 60% of tertiary-educated Caribbeans leave for opportunities in the U.S., the UK, or Canada.

For those who remain, the mismatch is glaring. Engineers drive taxis, teachers work at hotel front desks, and nurses juggle double shifts in underfunded hospitals. Parents invest everything in their children's schooling only to see them join the "can't see to can't see" grind in jobs unrelated to their training. Across the region, classrooms have multiplied, but futures have not. Secondary enrollment now exceeds 80% in Jamaica and the Bahamas, while Haiti, against staggering odds, has made significant progress toward universal primary education. Yet youth unemployment averages 25–30%, with young women suffering most.

The paradox deepens with higher education. In Jamaica, tertiary graduation rates have climbed to 20%, yet over 50% of skilled vacancies remain unfilled due to training mismatches. Degrees funnel graduates into call centers or tourism gigs, where wages often mirror those of high school jobs. The Bahamas, boasting a 90% secondary completion rate, mirrors the trap: despite education gains, youth unemployment stands at 15% in 2025, driven by tourism's seasonal fragility and the absence of diversified industries. Haiti suffers most: though primary enrollment surpasses 70%, quality remains uneven, leaving youth unemployment at 40%, fueled by instability and the scarcity of formal jobs.

This is not the failure of students but of systems built for dependency. Colonial education produced clerks for the empire; today's systems churn out graduates for service to foreign corporations or migration abroad. Women face a double burden, educated yet excluded, underpaid in feminized labor sectors, or pushed into informal economies. The cruel irony is clear: the younger people study, the less their societies can absorb them, and the conveyor belt of talent flows outward.

The salary crisis compounds this betrayal. In Jamaica, professionals earn some of the lowest wages in the region, around $1,200/month, barely enough to cover costs. In the Bahamas, seasonal jobs leave graduates idle during the off seasons, while in Haiti, political fragility collapses education gains into mass unemployment. Post-COVID setbacks widened these gaps further, leaving many young people with weak foundational skills and little chance of mobility.

These opportunity gaps are not incidental; they are engineered legacies of colonial underinvestment and modern dependency. Skills mismatches are glaring in St. Vincent, for example, 50% of vacancies remain unfilled not because youth lack degrees, but because training fails to align with technical needs. Simultaneously, overqualification pushes graduates into the informal sector or emigration, thereby draining local capacity.

Breaking this cycle requires reimagining education by aligning curricula with vocational and entrepreneurial opportunities, investing in innovation, and fostering industries that retain talent. Until then, the Caribbean's brightest will keep fleeing, and education will remain a promise unfulfilled.

Young People Leaving or Burning Out — Nowhere to Rise

Caribbean youth stand at a cruel crossroads: migrate in search of opportunity or stay and burn out at home. With unemployment hovering between 25% and 40% across the region, ambition feels more like a gamble than a pathway. Those who remain are often trapped in tourism jobs, call centers, or informal hustles,degrees reduced to credentials with no upward ladder.

The result is a hemorrhage of talent. More than 60% of tertiary-educated Caribbeans emigrate,the highest brain drain in the world. Jamaica loses nurses to Britain's NHS, Haiti loses engineers to Canada, and the Bahamas loses graduates to U.S. universities who rarely return. Communities are hollowed, families fractured, and economies starved of the very talent they invested in.

Those who stay often pay with exhaustion. With stagnant wages and rising costs, young workers juggle double shifts in Nassau's resorts or Kingston's call centers, laboring "from can't see to can't see" with little hope of advancement. Mental health crises mount, as depression and migration anxiety spread through a generation caught between survival and aspiration.

This isn't individual failure; it is structural sabotage. Colonial legacies denied land and ownership, while modern policies deny meaningful opportunity. Migration becomes survival, not ambition; burnout becomes the tax of loyalty to home. Governments often underinvest in mental health, while economic strategies frequently focus on fragile, low-wage sectors such as tourism and call centers.

The numbers are stark. Jamaica is projected to lose as much as 85% of its skilled workforce by 2025. In the Bahamas, where youth unemployment hovers near 20%, remittances sustain households. Still, at the cost of hollowing out local talent. Haiti's crisis is even sharper: amid political instability, thousands flee each year by boat, through borders, or into asylum systems leaving behind a development vacuum.

The toll on those who remain is both economic and psychological. Chronic underemployment breeds despair, "hustle fatigue," and disillusionment with systems that promise education but deliver stagnation. Innovation stalls, birth rates decline, and entire societies are locked in cycles of lack.

This dual crisis departure abroad, burnout at home was not accidental. It is the aftershock of colonial structures reinforced by modern dependency. Until Caribbean nations claim ownership of their futures through tech hubs, creative industries, agriculture, and green energy the brightest lights will continue to dim or depart, leaving entire generations stranded with nowhere to rise.

Nowhere to Rise: Youth Scattered or Shattered

Structural barriers keep Caribbean youth locked in place. Nepotism, limited startups, and tourism's dominance in low-skill work stifle upward mobility, even as youth dialogues in 2025 demand solutions to stem the brain drain. In Jamaica, the lowest salaries in the region accelerate departures, transforming would-be leaders into diaspora statistics. The cycle feeds itself: as talent flees, economies weaken, creating even fewer opportunities at home. Those who stay face burnout, trapped in precarious jobs that corrode ambition and mental health.

Yet the way forward is visible. **Youth-led initiatives tech hubs, green enterprises, creative industries **offer rungs where none exist, crafting ladders out of stagnation. Breaking the cycle requires more than survival: it requires ownership.

Modern labor in the Caribbean is not a paradise postcard it is a battleground. Tourism leeches' wealth, education mocks ambition, and youth either scatter abroad or shatter in burnout. From Bahamian beaches to Haitian hills, this grind demands revolt: owning stakes in tourism, aligning schools with local industries, and building opportunities at home. Only then can the region's young people open their eyes not to endless labor, but to destinies that rise beyond survival.

Caribbean youth face an economy with few ladders and many traps. Nepotism, limited access to capital, and an overreliance on tourism confine opportunity to low-skill, low-wage work, even as young people demand change. In countries like Jamaica, stagnant wages and scarce advancement accelerate migration, draining communities of talent and leadership. Those who remain are often caught in precarious employment, where burnout replaces ambition and mental health deteriorates under the weight of stalled futures.

Still, paths forward are emerging. Youth-led ventures in technology, renewable energy, agriculture, and the creative economy are carving out alternatives to dependency, proving that innovation can thrive when paired with ownership. These efforts challenge the assumption that success requires departure and demonstrate that the region's future does not have to be outsourced. What is missing is scale,investment, policy support, and access to capital that allow these initiatives to grow beyond survival.

The stakes are existential. When opportunity is absent, youth either scatter abroad or fracture at home, carrying the costs in lost potential and fractured communities. Reversing this trajectory demands structural change: ownership within tourism, education aligned with local industries, and economies built for value creation rather than extraction. Only then can Caribbean youth move from endurance to elevation, inheriting not exhaustion, but the power to rise.

PART FOUR

THE COST OF NEVER ARRIVING

Chapter 11

THE TOLL ON THE BODY AND SPIRIT

The grinds does not merely consume hours it consumes people. Piece by piece, it devours body and spirit, leaving scars that stretch across generations. In the relentless rhythm of "from can't see to can't see," Black communities from the Carolinas to The Caribbean carry the embodied cost of centuries: stress calcified into hypertension, trauma encoded in DNA, and spirits frayed by the weight of survival.

This is not ordinary fatigue. It is a systemic assault, where history's chains resurface as chronic disease in Charleston nurses, burnout in Nassau hotel staff, or depression in Kingston entrepreneurs. The hustle, so often glorified as resilience, disguises a harsher truth: our labor has been purchased at the price of our health and wholeness.

To reckon honestly, we must count the toll shortened lives, fractured minds, inherited wounds, endless exhaustion. And then, we must do more: demand ownership of healing, reclaiming the rest, vitality, and vision that the grind has stolen for too long.

Chronic Stress, Mental Health, Inherited Trauma

Chronic stress is not weakness it is history carried in the body. For Black people in the Carolinas, the Caribbean, and across the diaspora, stress is less an individual flaw than a racial inheritance, rooted in centuries of enslavement, colonialism, and systemic exclusion. It manifests today as mental health crises that echo unhealed wounds from generations past.

In the United States, systemic racism heightens exposure to trauma, leaving Black Americans more likely to develop PTSD after violent or destabilizing events. This "toxic stress" corrodes well-being daily, linking directly to health disparities: higher risks of depression, anxiety, and hypertension. Yet healthcare systems too often compound the harm Black patients face overdiagnosis of schizophrenia, underdiagnosis of mood disorders, and stigma that labels mental health struggles as weakness rather than a survival's scar.

The weight extends beyond the individual. Inherited trauma intergenerational trauma passes silently through families. The aftershocks of slavery, Jim Crow, colonial exploitation, and persistent discrimination alter epigenetics, shaping risks for both mental and physical illness across generations. Anxiety, depression, hypertension, and even shortened life expectancy are not just personal battles, but the biological imprint of historical violence.

This is the hidden toll of the grind: trauma doesn't fade when ignored; it multiplies, embedding itself into DNA, reshaping futures until we confront and heal it collectively.

INHERITED TRAUMA ACROSS THE DIASPORA

In the Carolinas, the legacy of isolation carried by Gullah-Geechee descendants emerges today as elevated mood disorders, intergenerational trauma, and heightened rates of domestic violence wounds compounded by limited access to culturally competent care. Across the Caribbean, colonial scars intertwined with modern pressures of poverty and instability. In Jamaica and the Bahamas, economic stagnation collides with stigma so pervasive that 63% of Black people view mental illness as personal weakness, delaying care and deepening unspoken wounds.

Haiti's struggle is even more acute: earthquakes, political upheaval, and relentless poverty stack atop ancestral trauma, leaving youth with PTSD rates far above global averages. Their spirits are weighed down by inherited survival modes, hypervigilance, mistrust of systems, and chronic anxiety passed like heirlooms through generations.

This cycle is not biology alone; it is the shadow of structural racism. Black communities across the diaspora endure "weathering" the accelerated aging of body and mind under the constant strain of discrimination and survival. This weather shortens lifespans, erodes resilience, and demands that healing itself be understood as a form of resistance, a reclamation of life against centuries of theft.

HOW THE CONSTANT HUSTLE BREAKS THE BODY

The hustle relentless, glorified, inescapable doesn't build empires for Black folk; it breaks us down, cell by cell, until the grind itself becomes a slow-acting poison. What the world calls resilience often manifests in chronic disease, physical breakdown, and premature death across the diaspora.

Lack of sleep, poor nutrition, and unending stress translate into skyrocketing rates of hypertension, diabetes, and cardiovascular disease. Hustle culture fuels coping through increased alcohol and substance use, while the physical signs of "hustle fatigue" emerge as chronic fatigue, back pain, chest tightness, and weakened immunity. Over time, the body buckles under the strain.

In the Carolinas, Black workers tied to warehouses, farms, and service jobs report higher rates of musculoskeletal disorders from long shifts and heavy labor. At the same time, accelerated aging, also known as weathering, carves stress into their very DNA. In the Caribbean, hotel maids who clean dozens of rooms daily, or taxi drivers on the road from dawn to midnight, often develop joint problems, respiratory conditions, and immune fragility decades before their time.

The grind doesn't just demand sweat it exacts years, shaving lifespans through exhaustion masked as ambition. Every sunrise clocked in, every night shift endured, leaves another scar on the body, until survival itself becomes a health crisis.

The Caribbean, comprising diverse nations such as Jamaica, the Bahamas, Barbados, St. Vincent, and St. Lucia, reflects a shared history of labor exploitation that continues to shape the lives of its people. In Jamaica, the seasonal tourism grind wears down workers maids breathe in harsh chemicals in stuffy, poorly ventilated rooms, bartenders endure grueling double shifts, and bellmen strain their backs with heavy loads, all while exhaustion becomes a daily reality. Respiratory illnesses take hold where safety measures are scarce, and burnout not only frays patience but erodes physical health, layering chronic conditions onto the economic desperation that demands relentless labor. In the Bahamas, the tourism-driven economy pushes hotel staff to their limits with long hours and little rest. This vulnerability was laid bare during past crises, such as the pandemic.

Barbados mirrors this strain, where the tourism and hospitality sectors demand intense effort from workers housekeepers' scrub tirelessly in hot conditions, waitstaff juggle crowded shifts, and groundskeepers toil under the sun, often with inadequate breaks. The physical toll includes muscle fatigue and heat-related ailments, compounded by a system that prioritizes profit over well-being, leaving workers caught in a cycle of overwork and undercard.

In St. Vincent, the reliance on agriculture and tourism creates a dual burden farm laborers bend over crops in humid fields, risking joint pain and dehydration. In contrast, tourism workers in hotels face similar overwork, with cleaners and porters pushing through exhaustion to meet seasonal demands. Safety nets are thin, and the lack of proper rest fosters a culture of endurance that silently damages health.

St. Lucia's picturesque landscapes hide a similar struggle, where tourism employees' housekeepers inhaling cleaning fumes, cooks standing for hours, and tour guides managing large groups face physical wear from repetitive tasks. The absence of robust health protections allows fatigue and stress-related illnesses to take root, reinforcing a cycle where economic necessity drives workers beyond their limits, echoing the region's historical labor scars.

Across these islands, the legacy of exploitation persists, with bodies bearing the cost of an economy that demands more than it sustains. Yet, within this struggle lies a resilient spirit where communities are beginning to demand fair labor practices, weave safety nets, and reclaim their well-being, offering a glimmer of hope for a future where the chains of the past no longer dictate their present.

Science confirms what communities have long suspected: chronic overwork can rewire the body. It floods systems with cortisol, disrupts hormones, inflames organs, and accelerates cellular aging. Across the diaspora, Black populations face two to three times higher rates of stress-linked illnesses like hypertension, diabetes, and cardiovascular disease, a brutal convergence of poverty and racism.

This isn't resilience, it's erosion. The grind, disguised as survival, chips away at vitality, leaving bodies broken and spirits dimmed. It is the direct inheritance of systems that value Black labor while disregarding Black life.

NO REST. NO SAFETY. NO VISION.

This is the invisible architecture of oppression that spans the streets of Charleston, the resorts of Nassau, the markets of Kingston, and the alleyways of Port-au-Prince. Rest, safety, and vision are not luxuries; they are the raw materials of healing, creativity, and forward momentum. Yet for Black communities across the diaspora, these materials are systemically withheld.

Without rest, the body fractures cells inflamed, hearts overworked, lives cut short.

Without safety, there is no sanctuary homes that become stress chambers, jobs become battlegrounds, and hospitals become sites of neglect.

Without vision, communities are trapped in the fog of survival, unable to imagine or build beyond the next paycheck, the next shift, or the next crisis.

What emerges is a generational state of exhaustion. Fatigue becomes inheritance. Hustle becomes culture. Grind becomes glorified trauma.

The receipts are clear: Black Americans die earlier and sicker, disproportionately from stress-driven illnesses like hypertension, diabetes, and heart disease. Maternal mortality among Black women remains a national disgrace, three to four times higher than for white women. Mental health care remains fractured, stigmatized, and inaccessible. Caribbean nations mirror this cruelty: Bahamian and Jamaican hospital wards overflow with untreated chronic illness, while Haitian clinics strain under trauma compounded by disaster.

These outcomes are not anomalies. They are the design. A system that weaponizes fatigue and withholds care ensures that "from can't see to can't see" is not just a workday it's a life sentence.

Geography compounds the disparities. In the Carolinas, the lingering legacy of redlining and segregation creates neighborhoods where safety is conditional, and rest is perpetually interrupted by poverty, violence, and systemic disinvestment. Upward mobility here is not just elusive, it is deliberately obstructed.

Across the Caribbean, the accents shift, but the oppression feels the same. In Trinidad and Tobago, an energy-rich economy still fails to shield working-class citizens from volatility, underemployment, and inflation. In Barbados, the pursuit of tourism-driven growth comes at the cost of worker exhaustion and the quiet erosion of culture. In Saint Lucia and Dominica, climate disasters force communities into endless cycles of rebuilding, denying rest and dimming collective vision. In Grenada, the echoes of political upheaval linger, tethering safety to scarce economic opportunity that drives young people abroad. In Jamaica and the Bahamas, the absence of safety nets pushes youth into burnout or migration, leaving behind hollowed-out communities. And in Haiti, crisis is constant, political instability, foreign interference, and natural disasters saturate the soil with trauma, where rest is a luxury, safety a gamble, and vision itself an act of rebellion.

Whether in Charleston or Kingston, Nassau or Port-au-Prince, the pattern repeats: Black labor is consumed, Black rest is denied, Black futures are foreclosed. Geography may draw borders, but the grind recognizes none.

Across the diaspora, these conditions converge into dangerous inheritance. When rest is denied, the body collapses. When safety is absent, trust corrodes. When vision is stolen, innovation withers. What remains is a brutal cycle of poverty, hyper-vigilance, and despair passed down like unwanted heirlooms, worn heavy on each new generation.

These are not abstractions; they are lived wounds. They are the aching backs bent over Charleston kitchens, the weary eyes straining through double shifts in Port of Spain, the stifled dreams shuttered behind doors in Kingston, Nassau, Bridgetown, and Castries.

Yet even in this void, the soil remains fertile enriched by struggle, watered with tears, seeded with resistance, and sustained by unyielding hope. The very systems that have broken our backs and bruised our spirits have also revealed what must be rebuilt. To reclaim rest in such a world is not leisure it is rebellion. It refuses to measure worth by output or to exchange our bodies for crumbs of validation. It is declaring that our humanity is not conditional, that we are more than what we produce, and that rest is not the prize of exhaustion, it is our birthright.

Rebuilding safety is not simply a policy goal; it is a spiritual charge and a communal mission. Safety is not the barbed wire of policing or the illusion of gated walls it is the heartbeat of trust that binds us together. It is children walking to school without fear, women whose voices are heard and protected, elders whose wisdom is honored, and communities where joy is not criminalized but celebrated. To rebuild safety is to mend the sacred fabric of our neighborhoods, to weave back the threads that centuries of violence, poverty, and neglect have unraveled. It requires ecosystems of care where justice is visible, trust is currency, and harm is met not with silence or erasure but with restoration and repair.

Reclaiming rest must also stand at the center of liberation. Rest is not laziness, it is resistance. It is the radical act of refusing to measure our worth solely by output or to sacrifice our bodies for survival crumbs. Rest is the declaration that Black life is valuable beyond productivity. It is Sabbath for weary souls, breath for generations that have been smothered, and the soil where creativity and healing can finally take root. Without rest, safety cannot hold. Without rest, vision cannot grow.

Reviving vision, then, is the sacred labor of this generation. As it is said, "Without vision, the people perish." Vision is not optional, it is urgent. It is a refusal to accept survival as our ceiling. It is the courage to imagine a future where our communities are not scattered by migration or crushed by poverty but flourishing in dignity, ownership, and joy. Vision is not abstract, it is practice. It means teaching our children to dream audaciously, equipping our youth to lead boldly, and daring to see ourselves as more than victims of history. To dream in full color is to resist the gray cage of oppression.

Together, rest, safety, and vision form the unshakable trinity of freedom. Rest restores the body, safety secures the soul, and vision directs the future. If one is missing, we are left vulnerable. But when they converge, they create the foundation for a people who will not merely survive but rise with eyes open, unbroken, and unafraid.

We cannot afford to pass down only the wounds, the scars, and the fatigue. We must also pass down the blueprints for liberation the strategies of survival turned into systems of thriving. The songs and prayers of our ancestors must become not just memories, but instruction. The rituals of healing, the languages of resistance, and the courage to dream outside the cage, these are the inheritances we must fight to preserve. To own our healing is to break the chain of suffering mid-link. To build systems of rest and protection is to raise scaffolding strong enough for generations to climb higher. And to dream without apology is to declare to the world that our presence is no accident, it is purposeful, it is divine, it is necessary.

We do not betray our ancestors by daring to rest. We honor them. We honor them by completing the freedom work they began not only with fists and marches, but with gentler hands that plant seeds, with clearer minds that envision alternatives, with softer hearts that make room for joy. They endured so we might do more than endure.

True freedom will never be found in the machinery of endless labor. It will not come from grinding ourselves into dust or mistaking exhaustion for progress. Freedom begins in rest, where the soul exhales and remembers its worth. It takes root in safety, where the body breathes without fear. And it blossoms in vision, where imagination breaks the walls of survival and opens into unshackled futures.

This is the inheritance we owe: not just pain carried forward, but possibility carved open. To rest is resistance. Building safety is a revolution. To dream is the purest rebellion. And to live fully beyond survival's veil is to finally arrive where our ancestors pointed all along: toward freedom that heals, restores, and endures.

PART FIVE

BREAKING THE CYCLE

Chapter 12

REST IS REVOLUTIONARY

The cycles will not break with more hustle. It will not shatter with longer hours, extra shifts, or multiple side hustle. It breaks only when we dare to stop. To breathe. To pause. To reclaim the sacred stillness that was stolen from us long before we were born.

In a world that demands Black bodies stay in motion grinding from dawn's first whisper to night's final sigh rest emerges as rebellion. It is not leisure. It is not laziness. It is revolution. Rest is insubordination against empires and economies that depend on our exhaustion. It is a refusal to let capitalism chew through our bones and spit us out nameless, faceless, and spent.

From the weary porches of the Carolinas to the sunbaked streets of Trinidad, Dominica, and Barbados where the legacy of "from can't see to can't see" bound generations in invisible chains rest calls us to revolt. It is the heartbeat of refusal, the unspoken language of dignity.

Our ancestors understood this truth. Even in the fields, they carved resistance into stolen minutes humming spirituals under their breath, rocking children to sleep with lullabies that carried hope, and whispering prayers into the midnight wind. In the silence between the cracks of songs, they sowed seeds of rebellion. Rest was their hidden weapon, their way of reclaiming fragments of a humanity that slavery and colonialism tried to erase.

Now, in our generation, rest is the inheritance we are reclaiming. To lie down without guilt is to defy centuries of lies that told us our worth was measured in labor. To close our eyes and dream is to write blueprints for freedom. To rise slowly, without panic, is to remind the world that we are not machines, we are divine.

Rest is not passive. It is power. It is preparation. It is the fertile soil where vision grows. Without it, exhaustion becomes the enemy of imagination. With it, we remember that our future is not bound to survival, but to flourishing.

To rest is to revolt. To rest is to resist. To rest is to return to us, to our ancestors, to the rhythm of life that says we were made not only to work, but to be.

The Nap Ministry and Black Rest Theology

In my book A New Star in Business, I introduced the idea that success is incomplete without wholeness that true achievement is not measured solely by what we accumulate outwardly, but by how we remain aligned inwardly. I argued then, as I argue now, that without rest, even the most dazzling accomplishments collapse under their own weight. Later, in Success: The Total Package, I urged readers to dismantle toxic definitions of productivity, not as perpetual output, but as intentional, purpose-filled effort that leaves sacred space for the soul to breathe. Those earlier works were seeds of the revelation this chapter now shouts aloud: rest is not an interruption to greatness it is the ground it grows from.

The Nap Ministry crystallizes this truth. Founded in 2016 by Tricia Hersey, the self-proclaimed "Nap Bishop," it began as performance art and has swelled into a global movement. Hersey's 2022 bestseller Rest Is Resistance and her 2025 follow-up We Will Rest! The Art of Escape reframed rest as reparations an embodied refusal to be consumed by grind culture and white supremacy. Through Instagram meditations, Patreon communities, and collective rituals of pausing, she calls us to "stay open to love" and step out of the machinery that seeks to commodify every breath and bone.

This is more than advocacy. It is a theology. Rooted in Black theology and womanist thought, Hersey draws on the lineage of liberation voices, such as James Cone, who declared God to be always and forever on the side of the oppressed. In this frame, rest itself becomes holy defiance. It proclaims that divinity is not revealed in endless busyness, but in the breath, in the stillness that refuses to be swallowed by empire.

And across the diaspora, this resonates with echoes older than the Atlantic crossing itself. The Gullah-Geechee of the Carolinas sang spirituals that doubled as coded prayers for freedom and rest. Lucian proverbs, Bahamian bush rituals, and Jamaican folk wisdom all preserved rhythms of restoration, pauses of soul-tending during survival. Long before we had academic language for "rest as resistance," our ancestors modeled it: carving Sabbath into silence, stealing naps in fields, braiding healing into hair and song.

Rest, in this light, is not just recovery. It is remembrance. It is how we remember who we were before we were reduced to workers, before our worth was measured in output, before our humanity was stripped down to labor. It is how we remember that we were always whole, always sacred, always more than what was extracted from us.

Rest as Resistance in Capitalism

Let us be clear: rest is a form of rebellion. Within the machinery of capitalism especially its colonial, plantation-birthed form Black rest is dangerous. It undermines the system because it refuses to feed it. On the plantation's, enslaved Africans were driven "from can't see to can't see," their value reduced to labor extracted until the body broke. That logic never died; it simply evolved into wage slavery, service economies, and gig platforms that still measure us by hours and output.

Tricia Hersey, the Nap Bishop, names this plainly: "Grind culture is a spiritual crisis." Capitalism trains us to believe that our worth is our productivity, that exhaustion is a badge of honor, and that silence in suffering is maturity. It thrives on Black fatigue,not by accident, but by design. Our overwork is expected, normalized, and monetized. Every weary shift in a Charleston warehouse, every double duty in a Nassau resort, every gig run on tired legs through Kingston's streets continues the same extraction pattern.

And yet rest disrupts it. To lie down, to pause, to reclaim stillness in a culture that demands our endless motion is nothing less than insubordination. Rest interrupts the cycle. It dismantles the myth. It says: my breath cannot be priced, my peace cannot be taxed, and my body cannot be owned. It is a declaration that humanity is not up for sale.

Rest, then, is more than recovery it is resistance. It is how we rebel against the plantation ghosts that linger in cubicles, call centers, and hotel kitchens. It is how we refuse to be consumed. Every nap, every pause, every act of self-preservation becomes a protest, a revolutionary refusal to be devoured by systems built on our exhaustion.

This reality is not abstract it is etched into our bloodlines and bone memory. It is what inspired the title of this very book. The phrase, whispered across generations in Black households, described a day's work that began before the first glimmer of dawn and did not end until darkness once again swallowed the land. At one level, it was a simple description of time. But at its core, it was a spiritual indictment of a testimony against systems that demanded our bodies be in perpetual motion, that measured our worth by our exhaustion, that allowed no pause, no peace, and no protection.

This phrase is more than an idiom. It is a mirror of history itself. It recalls the enforced labor of the plantation, where enslaved Africans worked under the lash until their bodies gave way. It lingers in the Reconstruction era, where sharecroppers bent their backs from sunrise to sunset, never escaping debt or dependency. It echoes in the 20th-century South, where Black women rose before daybreak to clean white households, and in Northern cities where Black men took graveyard shifts on factory lines. It carries into our own time, in fast-food counters, nursing homes, call centers, warehouses, and gig apps every space where Black and brown labor is extracted without reprieve.

"From can't see to can't see" is not just about time it is about inheritance. It is about how overwork became normalized, how survival became ritual, how motion was passed down while rest was denied. It is about how we learned to keep moving, because stopping meant risking hunger, eviction, or violence. It is about how entire communities were taught that our only value was in what we could produce.

And yet, by naming it, we expose it. By remembering the weight of this phrase, we refuse to let it define our future. It has been the story of our past, then rest, reclamation, and restoration must be the story we write next.

In a system born of plantations and refined by capitalism, rest becomes rebellion. Black labor has long been measured by exhaustion "from can't see to can't see" first under the lash, later through wages, contracts, and algorithms that disguise extraction as opportunity. Grind culture, as Tricia Hersey names it, is a spiritual crisis that equates worth with productivity. To rest is to refuse that inheritance, to declare that our bodies are not commodities and our humanity is not for sale. Rest is not retreating it is resistance.

From the Grind to the Quiet Revolution

Across the diaspora, the legacy of endless labor continues to unfold before our eyes. In the gig economies of the Carolinas, contract work carries the ghost of sharecropping apps replacing overseers yet still demanding unbroken toil for meager returns. In the all-inclusive resorts of Saint Lucia, Antigua, and the Bahamas, workers pour drinks, change linens, and smile for guests while masking their own exhaustion, their bodies fueling an industry that rarely invests in their futures. In Jamaica's under-resourced schools, where teachers labor for salaries that cannot sustain their families, and in Trinidad's factories where the industrial grind robs both time and health, the story repeats. Even in the hidden labor behind every tourist photo, cruise itinerary, and beachfront escape, Black and brown bodies remain the backbone of systems that profit off our sweat but seldom pour back into our lives.

Still, we grind. Still, we press. Still, we work from "can't see to can't see," clinging to the belief that the hustle will one day deliver us, that sacrifice today guarantees stability tomorrow. But the truth has borne out in generations of evidence that this promise is a mirage. The hustle, without rest, cannot save us.

And yet, a new rhythm is rising.

Through Afrofuturist dreaming, through digital soul care practices, through a widening theology of healing, new generations are daring to choose a different path. They are daring to imagine lives not defined by exhaustion, but by wholeness. Black women, in particular, are leading this quiet revolution reclaiming boundaries, naming burnout, practicing joy, and teaching that rest is not a side note to resistance but a central strategy. It is sanctuary. It is protest.

As Tricia Hersey reminds us, "Rest is not a luxury. It's resistance." To pause in a system that thrives on our depletion is to disrupt it. To sleep when capitalism demands our motion is to rebel. To dream when oppression only offers survival is to lay claim to futures that are ours by birthright.

We rest not to abandon the struggle, but to remember what we are fighting for. We rest not to avoid work, but to realign ourselves with the deeper work of becoming whole, individually and collectively. In this way, rest becomes our blueprint, our shield, and our inheritance reclaimed.

Returning to Sabbath as Spiritual Protest

The Sabbath is not nostalgia it is resistance. It is a return to divine rhythm, a cadence older than empire, older than capitalism, older than colonial chains. It is God's reminder etched into creation itself: "On the seventh day, God rested" not out of fatigue, but to set a boundary, to declare that constant toil is not divine, it is destructive.

For enslaved Africans in the Carolinas and the Caribbean, Sabbath was never merely a doctrine to recite it was a dream to embody. Even when denied rest by overseers and masters, they carved out holy pauses in stolen hours of song, whispered prayers, and communal meals after brutal days. Sabbath, in this context, was not a matter of compliance; it was a matter of rebellion. It was saying: "You may own my labor, but you cannot own my soul."

In Black theology, the Sabbath is a symbol of liberation. Just as God commanded Israel to rest as a testimony that they were no longer Pharaoh's slaves, so too does Sabbath announce to Black communities: we are not machines, we are not disposable, we are not property. To embrace rest is to resist the plantation logic that says our worth is in production.

In today's world, Sabbath is more than a "day off." It is a political act. To shut laptops, silence phones, and refuse the endless pull of hustle culture is to defy capitalism's demand for our exhaustion. It is to live out what Tricia Hersey calls "rest as resistance" a protest rooted not in idleness, but in reclamation of our humanity.

Across the diaspora, Sabbath practices are rising again not always on Sunday, but in deliberate rituals of pause. A digital Sabbath, where phones are put down. A family Sabbath, where joy and meals replace hustle. A personal Sabbath, where naps become sacraments. These practices echo ancient truths: that rest is sacred, that rest is communal, that rest is revolutionary.

To return to Sabbath is to declare: we were not made for endless grind. We were made for wholeness. And in reclaiming Sabbath, we protest every system that tries to convince us otherwise.

Sabbath as Heritage and Survival

In the Carolinas, Black churches have long made the Sabbath more than just worship it was a sanctuary carved out of struggle, a place for wellness. Sunday was the day when kitchens became communion tables, choirs became therapy, and the sanctuary became a shield against a hostile world. For many, it was the only day when the body could slow down, the mind could breathe, and the soul could imagine a life beyond the fields, factories, or service jobs waiting on Monday morning. Sabbath was a form of resistance because it reminded us that we were more than just workers we were whole.

Across the Caribbean, this heritage endures. In Barbados and Guyana, elders still insist on Sunday silence: shops close, radios dim, and younger generations are reminded that rest is not laziness but legacy. To pause is to honor the ancestors who could not. To rest is to claim back what was stolen. These cultural rituals, sometimes subtle, sometimes fiercely protected, are acts of resistance in a region still struggling under the weight of tourism's pressures and economic precarity.

And in Haiti, where survival often overshadows stillness, the Sabbath assumes a different meaning. Political upheaval, foreign exploitation, and natural disasters have made rest feel like a luxury. Yet even there, the hunger for pause remains. In 2024, during one of Haiti's most violent and uncertain periods, gang leader Jimmy "Barbecue" Chérizier declared, "Even though we are in a war, the weekend is the weekend." It was a chilling statement, but it revealed something profound: the human spirit refuses to surrender the need for rhythm, for pause, for Sabbath,even in chaos. Rest, in this context, is not softness. It is survival. It is order in disorder. It is humanity refusing to vanish.

The Sabbath, then, is not just ritual. It is a solid structure when all other systems collapse. It is memory when history tries to erase us. It is the audacity to say: we will not let oppression dictate the totality of our time. Across the diaspora, this truth rings clear rest is not only for the fortunate. It is for the weary, the wounded, the waiting. It is for us all.

Reclaiming Rhythm, Reclaiming Ourselves

In Grenada and Saint Vincent, Sabbath is not always found in pews it lives in the steaming pots of Sunday meals, in slow ocean walks, in the shade of breadfruit trees on family land. These are sacred pauses disguised as ordinary acts. Even in secular expressions digital detoxes, collective naps, sunrise meditations, or the discipline of silence before the world's noise,the spirit of Sabbath persists. It isn't about religious legalism. It isn't about nostalgia for another era. It is about rhythm. About choosing cadence over chaos, intention over urgency. It is about remembering that dignity does not come from endless motion, but from honoring stillness as a sacred thing.

We were never designed to be machines. The call to rest was not a suggestion, it was a commandment. The Jewish community has carried this truth for centuries, not as a hidden treasure but as a torch in plain sight, written into Torah, etched into the cosmic order of creation itself: "Remember the Sabbath day, and keep it holy." Not as restriction, but as liberation. Not as a law to bind, but as a rhythm to free. The Creator carved rest into the very DNA of the universe six days of work, one day of renewal not for one tribe alone, but as a universal whisper to all humanity: pause, be still, and remember you are not slaves to Pharaoh, to empire, to capitalism, to grind.

But somewhere along the way, we lost the plot. We outsourced Sabbath to others, assuming it was their inheritance and not ours. We reduced it to a ritual or relic, a custom for the "religious" but irrelevant to the weary. And in forgetting, we surrendered one of the most radical tools of liberation we had. Sabbath was never meant to be ornamental it was intended to be operational. It was always more than sleep or stopping. It was sanctifying time. It was drawing a holy boundary around our peace. It was remembering that we are not disposable, not merely units of output, not cogs in someone else's machine.

To reclaim Sabbath now is to rewrite the script. It is to say: our time is ours. Our rest is sacred. Our pause is a protest. And in choosing it, we return not just to dignity, but to divinity the God who rested, the ancestors who dreamed of rest, and the future generations who will inherit the rhythm we choose to restore today.

And yet, even when we ignored what was already written, the truth refused to stay hidden. Like scattered breadcrumbs left along humanity's journey, other faiths and philosophies picked up the refrain. Buddhism whispers that stillness awakens us to reality.

Rest as Cosmic Covenant

Confucian wisdom teaches that balance, retreat, and harmony form the foundation of a moral life. Islam gifts us Jummah Friday pause, prayer, and reconnection as a weekly rhythm of rest for the soul. Indigenous traditions across Africa, the Caribbean, and the Americas long centered rituals of pause, dance, and renewal as part of communal survival. Across continents, across languages, across centuries, the message keeps returning rest is not an indulgence it is a necessity for wholeness.

Rest, then, is not cultural it is cosmic. It is not tied to one people, one ritual, or one theology. It was woven into the first week of existence. Before there were empires to resist, before there were plantations to endure or systems to overthrow, there was a Creator who labored for six days and then rested. Not because of exhaustion, but as a revelation. As a rhythm. As a blueprint. As a covenant.

To rest is to align with God's order. To grind endlessly is to break from it. When we push our bodies past their limits, when we glorify exhaustion as if it were a badge of honor, when we teach our children that burnout equals success, we are not just harming ourselves. We are breaking the covenant with the creator itself. We are rejecting a divine pattern that was never meant to bind us, but to bless us.

This is why reclaiming rest is more than self-care, it is soul-care. It is the restoration of the covenant, a return to sanity in a world built on madness, a refusal to collude with the lie that our worth is measured by output. Rest becomes our way of stepping back into the sacred rhythm of the universe, declaring that our humanity is not disposable, and remembering what our ancestors already knew: we were never created to be machines we were created to be whole.

Rest as Revolutionary Return

Rest is revolutionary because it reclaims what was violently stolen: our time, our stillness, our divine spark. For centuries, systems of slavery, colonialism, and capitalism conspired to keep us in motion measured only by our output, valued only by our labor. To stop was to risk punishment. To rest was to invite erasure. And yet, across the Carolinas and throughout the Caribbean, our people still found ways to pause whether in stolen moments under a shaded tree, in whispered prayers before dawn, in the sacred silences of Sunday rituals, or in the rhythm of drums that called body and spirit back into alignment.

Today, that inheritance continues. From Tricia Hersey's prophetic nap ministries to our grandmothers' insistence on Sunday quiet, from James Cone's liberation theology to the pause-filled wisdom of elders in Dominica, Grenada, and Saint Vincent we see rest not as retreat, but as return. A return to ourselves. A return to wholeness. A return to the sacred rhythm that the empire tried to erase.

To rest is to remember. To pause is to resist. To breathe is to begin again. Each act of stillness becomes both a survival and a defiance: a refusal to let the grind dictate our worth, a refusal to let exhaustion be our legacy. This is not a trend,it is a torch. It is the flame passed from ancestor to descendant, illuminating the path toward a freedom where body, mind, and spirit can flourish.

And so, we reclaim rest not merely as resistance, but as revolution. We rise from "can't see to can't see" into a vision renewed, healing restored, and freedom finally within reach. Rest becomes our rebellion, our sanctuary, our strategy, and our song. It is where liberation begins because when we stop, we do not surrender. We return. We rise. We remember we were always meant to be free.

Chapter 13

THE NEW CRY FOR 40 ACRES

Freedom was never just about breaking chains. True freedom is ownership of land, of labor, of legacy. It is not merely the absence of oppression; it is the presence of power. Power to decide. Power to build. Power to pass on.

The cry for "40 acres and a mule" began as a whisper of hope on blood-soaked fields after the Civil War. It was never about charity it was about justice. It was not simply land, it was leverage. It was equity. It was the foundation of a future that should have been. Yet the promise was betrayed. Reconstruction gave way to Redemption, and the land was snatched back into the hands of those who once wielded the whip. Freedom was proclaimed, but without ownership, it was hollow. Without land, there was no security, no inheritance, no power.

That cry did not die. It has evolved, finding new tongues and new tones across centuries. Today, it resonates in the call for reparations in the United States, as well as in the demand for access to capital, the fight for business ownership, the securing of creative rights, and the reclaiming of land across the Caribbean. It is the cry of a people who say: we will no longer just work the land we will own it. We will no longer just labor we will lead. We will no longer just survive we will build; we will grow, we will leave something behind.

In the Carolinas, this struggle is ongoing. Gullah-Geechee descendants fight heirs' property laws that strip families of generational land, while developers circle like vultures. What was once refuge is now targeted as real estate. In the Caribbean, the story is the same with a different accent: in Jamaica, hillsides remain in the hands of elites; in the Bahamas, beachfronts belong to tourists while family land is entangled in disputes and debt; in Haiti, fertile soil lies fallow under the weight of foreign interference and political instability. The pattern is clear: the land surrounds us, but too often, ownership escapes us.

And yet, a new generation is rising. In Charleston, Black-owned businesses revitalize historic districts once gutted by neglect. In Nassau, farmers' markets flourish with the fruits of sovereignty, as young Bahamians reclaim food security from imports. In Kingston, tech entrepreneurs are building hubs that export innovation rather than labor. In Port-au-Prince, grassroots cooperatives form safety nets where governments have failed. Across the diaspora, the old cry is being reborn not as a plea, but as a plan.

This is the new cry for 40 acres: ownership as a form of resistance. Entrepreneurship as revolution. Sovereignty as survival. Freedom, in this vision, is no longer measured by how long we can endure someone else's system it is measured by how fully we can create our own.

This chapter is not a whisper. It is an unapologetic call to return to the table of promise not as beggars asking for scraps, but as builders laying down foundations. Employment alone will never be enough. Jobs, no matter how plentiful, cannot repair generations of theft. Wages cannot substitute wealth. Equity, not access, must be the measure.

True freedom demands more than participation in someone else's system. It requires ownership of the systems that sustain our lives. It calls us to move beyond survival wages into legacy wealth structures that endure, protect, and multiply.

That means cooperative economics, where communities pool resources to build credit unions, housing cooperatives, and shared enterprises that shield us from predatory systems. It means land trusts, where Black families safeguard property from heirs' property loopholes and displacement, ensuring that soil passes from ancestor to descendant without interruption. It means royalties and creative rights because in a digital age, our stories, art, and innovations must no longer be exploited, but monetized and controlled by us. It means estate planning, so that wealth is not swallowed by courts but secured for the generations yet unborn. And it means digital ownership, blockchain, NFTs, intellectual property rights as the new frontier of sovereignty, ensuring that our presence in the digital economy is not as laborers but as leaders.

We must also redefine wealth itself. Wealth is not just money, it is power. It is presence. It is permanence. It is the ability to decide where your family lives, how your children learn, and what legacy your name carries. It is the security of knowing you do not just belong in the world,you own part of it.

Because true freedom is not permission it is possession. It is not merely being allowed to live it is being empowered to own. It is not just breaking the chains it is owning the land those chains once dragged us across.

The cry for ***40 acres*** is no longer about acreage alone it is about agency. It is about transforming "from can't see to can't see" into a vision that stretches across generations. It is about building lives no longer rooted in survival, but in sovereignty.

Land, Business, and Generational Control

Ownership is not abstract, it is tangible, visible, and essential. It is the soil under our feet, the storefronts on our streets, and the legacies written into our wills. For the Black diaspora, ownership is not just about possession, it is about reversing centuries of systemic dispossession and rewriting the script of survival into a narrative of sovereignty.

LAND AS FOUNDATION

Land is the original wealth. It roots families, sustains food, and anchors culture. Without land, we remain at the mercy of landlords, developers, and foreign powers. With land, we reclaim the ability to decide how space is used, how resources are shared, and how communities grow. From heirs' property protection in the Carolinas to family land preservation in the Bahamas, land ownership is not nostalgia it is strategy. It is the first step in ensuring that "from can't see to can't see" no longer describes labor for someone else's profit, but stewardship for our own people's future.

BUSINESS AS ENGINE

Business transforms ownership into movement. It is the engine that generates jobs, circulates money, and funds dreams. But for too long, Black labor has built empires without a stake in their wealth. To shift this, we must move from employees to employers, from consumers to creators, from workers to wealth-builders. Cooperative businesses, tech startups, tourism ventures owned by locals, and creative enterprises powered by diaspora networks, these are not luxuries, they are necessities. Business ownership ensures that our communities are not just sites of labor but centers of power.

GENERATIONAL CONTROL AS FLAME

True freedom is measured not in years, but in generations. Generational control is the flame passed from ancestor to descendant, keeping vision alive across time. Estate planning shields property from predators. It is trusting funds and scholarships that give children more than a head start. It is cultural ownership stories, art, music that can never again be stolen or silenced. When we secure generational control, we ensure that freedom is not fragile but fortified. That our grandchildren inherit more than struggle, they inherit sovereignty.

Ownership, then, is not simply acquisition. It is reclamation. It is resistance. It is the blueprint for freedom that outlasts us. For when we own land, we own security. When we own businesses, we own the direction. When we control generations, we own the future itself.

Land as Foundation

Land is more than soil it is the bedrock of freedom. It holds memory, sustains life, and anchors communities in place. Without land, everything else becomes fragile.

In the United States, Black farmers have lost over **90% of their land since 1910,** stripped away through discriminatory lending, heirs' property disputes, and predatory partition sales. Once holding **14% of American farms,** Black ownership has fallen to just **1.4% today**. This was no accident it was a strategy. In the Carolinas, where rice and cotton plantations once enriched empires on the backs of enslaved Africans, land theft translated into stolen wealth, broken family ties, and uprooted communities. And yet, resistance continues in South Carolina, Gullah-Geechee families are reclaiming their heritage land through trusts and preservation initiatives that have already secured over 1,000 **acres,** ensuring sacred ground remains under community stewardship.

In the Caribbean, the story echoes. Colonial powers claimed the best lands for plantations, leaving Black and brown families with marginal plots or none. Today, tourism and foreign investors repeat the cycle. In Jamaica, hillside farmers struggle to secure titles, while beachfronts are fenced off by foreign-owned resorts. In the Bahamas, family land in places like Exuma often sits in legal limbo, vulnerable to developers who dangle quick cash. In Haiti, where foreign interests and political instability collide, landlessness perpetuates poverty and displacement.

Still, land is being reclaimed. Community farms in Kingston, eco-tourism initiatives in Dominica, and food-sovereignty movements across the region remind us that ownership is not nostalgia it is survival. To own land is to own the right to decide how space is used, how food is grown, and how culture is preserved.

Land remains the **foundation of sovereignty:** the difference between being perpetual tenants in someone else's empire and being architects of our own future. When we lose land, we lose anchor. When we reclaim land, we reclaim destiny.

If land is the foundation, business is the engine. It transforms survival into self-determination, fueling not only households but entire communities. Black-owned firms in the U.S. generate over **$200 billion annually;** yet, systemic barriers keep them locked out of growth pipelines, as only **0.2% of venture capital funding** flows to Black entrepreneurs. The message is clear our creativity is celebrated when it entertains but starved when it builds institutions.

And still, innovation thrives. In North Carolina, the revival of Durham's historic **Black Wall Street** has given birth to a new ecosystem of tech startups, cooperatives, and community-rooted enterprises. In Atlanta, the creative industries encompassing music, film, and fashion have become economic powerhouses, shaping culture while generating employment opportunities. In the Caribbean, Kingston's tech hubs, Nassau's small-business markets, and Port-au-Prince's grassroots cooperatives prove that entrepreneurship is not just about profit, it is survival, strategy, and sovereignty.

These ventures are not just businesses. They are **blueprints for freedom** engines that circulate wealth within Black communities, rather than letting it drain outward. Each storefront, farm, app, and cooperative is a defiance of centuries of extraction. Each one is a declaration: we will not only labor, but we will also lead.

Generational Control as Flame

The final piece of ownership is control across generations the flame that keeps freedom burning beyond one lifetime. Without succession planning, assets become fragmented, families feud, and legacies are lost. Today, the **median Black household holds only 15% of the wealth** of the median white household, a gap that widens every time land is lost or businesses fail to transfer intact.

Generational control is not just inheritance; it is intentional design. It is the creation of **trusts, will, land cooperatives, and estate plans** that turn fragile gains into permanent inheritance. It is the difference between children starting from zero and starting from a platform. It is the power to say: My sacrifice will not die with me.

In the Carolinas, some Gullah-Geechee families are using legal strategies to protect heirs' property from developers. In Jamaica, families are pooling remittances into collective businesses to ensure resources stay in local hands. In the Bahamas, new movements are emerging to establish family land trusts, aiming to safeguard cultural and economic legacies. These are not just financial tools, they are survival codes, ensuring that progress does not reset with every generation.

Generational control is more than possession, it is **continuity.** It is the assurance that land tilled by ancestors, businesses built by parents, and wealth earned through struggle will not evaporate but endure. It is not merely about passing something down, it is about passing something forward, lighting a flame that descendants can tend, expand, and carry into futures our ancestors could only have dreamed of.

Caribbean Parallels: Land, Business, and Resistance

The Caribbean tells a parallel story, one where land, business, and generational sovereignty remain both the promise and the battlefield. In Jamaica, post-independence land reform redistributed small plots, but the deeper inequity remained. Today, nearly **70% of prime coastal land** is owned by foreigners, with multinational tourism conglomerates fencing off beaches that once belonged to the local people. Locals now face displacement, inflated property prices, and the bitter irony of being guests on their own shores.

In The Bahamas, the story echoes with sharp clarity. Foreign investors control **as much as 80% of prime real estate,** especially along coveted coastlines, pricing Bahamians out of ancestral spaces that once carried memory and meaning. Yet, resistance endures. In Eleuthera, **community land trusts** protect Loyalist-era family plots, keeping Black Bahamian families rooted in their history and shielding them from speculative development that seeks to erase their presence.

In Haiti, the fight takes a different shape. Smallholder farmers who cultivate **60% of the nation's arable land** often lack formal titles, leaving them at the mercy of political upheaval, elite seizure, and foreign exploitation. Grassroots **peasant movements** demand agrarian reform, pushing back against centuries of dispossession and fighting to secure the soil that feeds their nation.

Business and entrepreneurship also pulse with promise across the region. In Jamaica, more than **1,000 registered startups** are reimagining the economy rooted in tech, food, and music, the same cultural engines that have long carried the island's influence worldwide. In Trinidad, creative industries drive export revenue. In the Bahamas, small-business markets in Nassau signal a quiet reclamation of sovereignty.

And yet, the cycle threatens to repeat itself. **Remittances from the diaspora,** while vital lifelines that fund homes, education, and local ventures, also reveal a dependence: communities relying on external flows rather than internal systems. Without structural reform policies that prioritize local ownership, protect heritage land, and establish equitable financing channels, foreign dominance and capital flight will continue to erode sovereignty, leaving Caribbean nations to struggle while outsiders reap the benefits.

Still, within these struggles lies a blueprint. Land trusts, cooperative enterprises, and diaspora-funded ventures point toward a future where ownership is reclaimed, not borrowed. The Caribbean's story is not just one of loss, it is one of resilience, where every act of protection, every startup, every reclaimed acre becomes a declaration: **we will not be strangers on our own land.**

Why Ownership, Not Job Placement, Is the True Path to Liberation

Job placement offers wages. Ownership delivers power.

This is the essential distinction in the struggle for liberation: **employment may provide survival, but ownership fosters autonomy, wealth, and a legacy.** Where jobs too often keep Black communities locked into dependency, ownership breaks chains and redefines freedom as control over one's labor, one's time, and one's destiny.

Even so-called "good jobs" reinforce hierarchy. In the United States, Black workers on average earn **76 cents for every dollar earned by white workers** (***U.S. Department of Labor,*** 2022). Job placement initiatives, often heralded as progress, frequently funnel Black workers into lower-wage, low-mobility sectors roles that sustain systems rather than transform them. A paycheck, no matter how steady, still relies on permission from someone else's table.

Ownership flips this equation. **Black-owned businesses, although underfunded, retain wealth within their communities for 8–10 times longer than the wages spent at outside corporations** (***Anderson, Power Nomics,*** 2001). This recirculation is not just an economic issue it is a matter of sovereignty. It means that every dollar becomes a seed, reinvested in schools, housing, and future enterprises, rather than being siphoned away.

History affirms this truth. From the rise and destruction of **Tulsa's Black Wall Street**[27] to the quiet resilience of Gullah-Geechee landholders in the Carolinas, liberation has always been tied to who owns the land, the store, the tools, and the rights. Job placement could never shield us from systemic shocks whether Depression-era layoffs, pandemic-era "essential expendability," or AI-driven job displacement in today's economy. Ownership, by contrast, offers resilience. When we own the farm, the firm, the digital platform, or the intellectual property, we hold the power to decide,not just to survive.

In the Caribbean, the lesson is just as clear. Bahamian hotel jobs pay wages, but foreign-owned resorts pocket the wealth. Jamaican call centers employ thousands, but the profits flow to multinational investors. Meanwhile, when local entrepreneurs reclaim agriculture, technology, or creative industries, the ripple effects uplift whole communities' ownership anchors sovereignty.

Liberation, then, is not found in access to someone else's payroll, it is found in building and controlling our own tables. Ownership transforms "from can't see to can't see" labor into a vision that stretches across generations. It replaces the instability of wages with the permanence of legacy. It is not charity. It is not placement. It is **power.**

27 Tulsa's Black Wall Street, the prosperous Greenwood District in Tulsa, Oklahoma, with over 600 Black-owned businesses, was destroyed in the 1921 Tulsa Race Massacre by a white mob, killing hundreds and leveling 35 blocks.

Ownership as Liberation in the Carolinas and the Caribbean

In the Carolinas, where gig work dominates and job insecurity reigns, the difference became undeniable during the 2020 pandemic shutdowns. Thousands of workers saw their jobs vanish overnight, restaurants closed, shifts canceled, gigs evaporated. But those who held even modest assets franchises, farmland, or rental property had buffers of stability that wage-earners did not. That gap is not simply a matter of luck. It is about structure. It is about ownership. As Angela Davis reminds us, **true freedom is not about integrating into systems of exploitation, but dismantling them altogether** (***Freedom Is a Constant Struggle***, 2016). Ownership is that dismantling in practice. It shifts the balance of power. It turns labor into leverage. It empowers bargaining, fuels innovation, and ensures legacy.

The Caribbean echoes this truth with painful clarity. In Jamaica, foreign-controlled tourism employs nearly **300,000 workers,** yet up to **80% of the revenue leaks abroad** into the hands of multinational corporations (UNWTO, 2019; Thomas, 2020). Jobs keep people afloat, but they do not build wealth they build dependency. In The Bahamas, "people-to-people" programs encourage cultural exchange, but liberation will not come from being tour guides for others. It will come when Bahamians own the resorts, the restaurants, and the excursion companies, keeping wealth within their communities rather than watching it drain away. In Haiti, cooperative farming models have already demonstrated the power of ownership: when farmers hold land collectively, productivity increases by **20–30%** (World Bank, 2018). Compare this with the sweatshop economy, where low-wage garment jobs perpetuate poverty and dependency while foreign investors extract the profits.

The lesson is unavoidable: **jobs can sustain, but they cannot liberate. Liberation** requires a shift from survival through wages to sovereignty through ownership. Whether it is land, business, or cooperative wealth, ownership is not just an economic strategy, it is the continuation of the freedom struggle by other means.

Ownership as the New Currency of Freedom

Ownership liberates because it does more than provide resources, it rewrites narratives, secures futures, and reshapes the balance of power. Jobs may sustain the body for a season, but ownership sustains the generations. It is the difference between wages that vanish at month's end and legacies that outlive us.

This is why the new cry for ***40 acres*** is not nostalgia, it is necessity. It is not about returning to an old promise but about insisting that freedom must be measured not by access to labor, but by control of land, business, and wealth. Ownership not placement, is the foundation of sovereignty. It transforms survival into stability, dependency into dignity, and labor into liberation.

When we own, we move from being expendable participants in someone else's economy to being architects of our own. We move from "can't see to can't see" into a vision that stretches across generations. We declare that our futures are not for sale, our resources are not disposable, and others will not write our stories. **Ownership is not the end of the struggle it is the beginning of a new freedom.**

Economic Models for Generational Wealth: UBI, Co-ops, Rotating Savings, and Land Trusts

Generational wealth isn't luck, it's strategy. It is the intentional design of systems that transform survival into sustainability, scarcity into sufficiency, and sufficiency into abundance. For Black communities across the Carolinas, the Caribbean, and the wider diaspora, wealth has too often been stripped away by theft, policy, and predatory systems. Rebuilding it requires more than individual hustle; it requires collective models rooted in both ancestral wisdom and radical innovation.

Across the diaspora, blueprints are emerging models such as Universal Basic Income (UBI), worker cooperatives, rotating savings associations, and land trusts. These are not abstract theories. They are practices born of necessity and sustained by culture, designed to ensure that what is earned is not just consumed in the moment, but preserved, multiplied, and passed forward.

- **Universal Basic Income (UBI):** Reimagines security by providing guaranteed financial floors, so survival is not dependent on precarious jobs or exploitative wages. For Black and Caribbean communities disproportionately trapped in low-wage labor, UBI is not charity, it is justice.
- **Cooperatives:** Whether farming co-ops in Haiti or credit unions in North Carolina, cooperatives pool resources to give communities ownership and decision-making power. They keep profits circulating locally, rather than bleeding outward.

- **Rotating Savings and Credit Associations (ROSCA/Susu/Partna):** These ancestral models, long practiced in West Africa and carried into the Caribbean, allow families to build capital collectively. They are trust-based economies that reject banks' gatekeeping and honor community accountability.
- **Land Trusts:** By placing land in collective stewardship, families and communities safeguard against dispossession, gentrification, and speculative development. In South Carolina's Gullah-Geechee corridors and Bahamian settlements, such as Eleuthera, land trusts are ensuring that heritage and homes remain in Black hands for generations to come.

These systems are not new they are continuations of existing ones. They echo the maroon settlements that pooled labor for survival, the market women who sustained economies outside colonial control, and the "sou-sou" networks that financed migration and mobility. They remind us that the path to generational wealth is not individual escape, but collective elevation.

True liberation will not come from waiting on the trickle-down of capitalism. It will come from building our own streams of income, of ownership, of inheritance that flow across generations.

Universal Basic Income (UBI): A Floor for Legacy

UBI is not a handout, it is a foundation for economic stability. It provides a floor beneath families, so they can stop living in free fall. In Stockton, California, the landmark $ 500-per-month pilot demonstrated what stability can make possible: Black participants experienced a 12% increase in full-time employment, debt burdens decreased, and small investments in education, transportation, and entrepreneurship became feasible. The lesson was clear when survival is no longer in question, possibilities multiply. Stability breeds mobility.

In the Carolinas, where wage stagnation and job insecurity still haunt Black communities, UBI could serve as a modern-day corrective to the broken promises of Reconstruction. Imagine if, instead of being funneled into cycles of underpaid gig work, families had a guaranteed income floor to invest in farmland, launch businesses, or simply breathe without fear of the next bill. That breathing room is not trivial it is the seedbed of innovation and legacy.

The Caribbean is also beginning to wrestle with this vision. In Jamaica, policy debates have circled around forms of income guarantees as unemployment and inflation surged in the mid-2020s. In Barbados, targeted supplements have been explored as buffers against the volatility of tourism, a sector that too often rises and crashes at the mercy of global markets. UBI in these contexts is not an abstract theory it is a form of survival insurance. It ensures that when hurricanes hit, when cruise ships stop docking, when remittances dry up, families don't collapse back into poverty.

Critics argue that UBI breeds dependency, but the evidence tells a different story. Rather than stripping ambition, it unlocks it. By stabilizing households, UBI prevents the constant backslide into debt that drains dreams before they can take hold. It transforms income from a stopgap into a steppingstone turning survival into sustainability and sustainability into a lasting legacy.

UBI, then, is more than a policy experiment. It is a form of reparative justice, a way of restoring stolen time, energy, and opportunities by giving Black and Caribbean families the margin to plan, create, and build. It says: our people deserve not just to survive the month, but to shape the century.

Universal Basic Income is not charity but infrastructure a floor that replaces constant economic free fall with stability.

For Black communities in the Carolinas and across the Caribbean, UBI offers a modern corrective to centuries of denied opportunity, providing breathing room in economies shaped by insecurity, tourism volatility, and climate shocks. By restoring time and choice, UBI transforms survival into sustainability and sustainability into legacy.

Cooperatives: Democracy in Ownership

Cooperatives are more than business models they are blueprints for shared survival and shared sovereignty. They democratize ownership by distributing both risk and reward across a community, ensuring that no single household bears the weight alone. For Black communities long excluded from traditional markets and capital, cooperatives have always been a way of saying: ***if they do not lend to us, we will lend to each other; if they will not sell to us, we will sell to each other.***

In the U.S., Black cooperatives generate over $500 million annually, a continuation of traditions that reach back to mutual aid societies of the 19th century. In the Carolinas, food hubs and farming cooperatives are reclaiming land and markets that were once stripped by discriminatory policies. By pooling resources, they preserve farmland, sustain small farmers, and keep profits circulating locally instead of bleeding into corporate chains. Every dollar stays in the soil of the community a little longer, nourishing more than just crops it nourishes dignity.

Across the Caribbean, cooperatives are lifelines rooted in ancestral wisdom. Jamaica's 200+ cooperatives from agricultural collectives to credit unions boost member incomes by as much as 25%, proving that shared risk produces shared strength. Haiti's farmer collectives have become a bulwark against climate shocks and market instability, ensuring that hurricanes or predatory buyers do not crush smallholders. In Trinidad, the credit union movement is one of the largest in the region, serving over 600,000 members. These unions make possible what commercial banks have long denied: access to loans, savings, and security. Guyana's rice and sugar co-ops reveal another truth when farmers move together, they can withstand the turbulence of global price swings better than any one family on its own.

This is not charity. It is power. Cooperative economics reclaims the ancient truth that many hands build stronger futures. Each member is both an investor and a beneficiary, as well as a laborer and a leader. In this model, wealth is not hoarded at the top it is shared in the circle.

Cooperatives, then, are not simply financial structures. They are cultural declarations. They remind us that freedom is not rugged individualism, but collective thriving. They turn survival into solidarity, and solidarity into sovereignty.

Rotating Savings: The People's Banks

Rotating savings systems-***sou, known as "Asue" in The Bahamas and Trinidad, partners in Jamaica, box hands in Barbados, or tontines*** in West Africa are the quiet engines of Black survival and sovereignty. They function with a simplicity that defies the bureaucracy of banks: each member contributes a set amount into a collective pot, and each cycle, one member takes the whole sum. With discipline and trust, what begins as small offerings becomes large, transformative lump sums, capable of funding businesses, weddings, funerals, land purchases, school fees, or migration journeys.

Across the diaspora, these "people's banks" remain among the most trusted tools for wealth building. In The Bahamas, "Asue'sou-sou groups often underwrite microenterprises, providing capital where banks refuse to lend. In Jamaica, partner plans are so institutionalized that some operate formally, offering returns of 10–15% a savings structure designed by the people, for the people. In Trinidad and Barbados, these systems are woven into the cultural fabric, a form of community insurance where the true collateral is reputation and trust.

Their origins run deep. During slavery and indenture, when Africans and Indians were denied access to land titles, loans, or wages that could accumulate, rotating savings became survival itself a shadow economy of resilience. These were not just financial instruments; they were acts of rebellion, networks of dignity in a world built to deny Black and brown people capital.

Today, they endure not as relics, but as proof that liberation economics need not wait for permission. Rotating savings systems bypass banks that still redline, exclude, or overcharge Black borrowers. They collapse the myth that only institutions can manage wealth. Instead, they remind us that community is the first bank, trust is the first currency, and reciprocity is the first investment strategy.

What began as a necessity has become a modern financial ecosystem. In every sou-sou, every partner hand, there is more than money circulating there is memory, discipline, and vision. These systems teach us that wealth is not hoarded; it is rotated, shared, and multiplied. They transform scarcity into sufficiency and remind us that freedom often begins with the simple act of pooling our resources and believing in one another.

Land Trusts: Securing Place and Heritage

Land is never just soil. It is memory. It is inheritance. It is the ground where our ancestors' footsteps echo and where our descendants will decide their futures. To lose land is not merely to lose property it is to lose place, belonging, and power. And yet, for centuries, Black communities across the diaspora have faced calculated dispossession: heirs' property disputes in the Carolinas, forced partition sales, and foreign land grabs in the Caribbean. The story is consistent, land slips through our hands while systems are built to ensure it is never fully ours.

Land trusts emerged as a shield against this ongoing theft. In the United States, Black-led land trusts now protect over 100,000 acres, reversing fragmentation and ensuring that heritage spaces remain in the hands of the community. In South Carolina, where Gullah-Geechee families have been pushed to the margins by predatory developers, community trusts safeguard sacred holdings, ensuring that the shoreline and farmland remain legacies, not commodities.

In the Caribbean, this fight takes a different but equally urgent form. In The Bahamas, community trusts are defending family islands against foreign speculation, protecting Loyalist-era holdings so that Bahamians retain access to their coastlines in a market where nearly 80% of prime beachfront is foreign-owned. In Grenada and Saint Lucia, new heritage land trusts are rising as bulwarks against resort expansion that threatens to erase fishing villages and uproot family homesteads.

But land trusts are not just defensive mechanisms, they are engines of permanence. They transform fragility into endurance. They turn scattered plots into sanctuaries. They ensure that land remains a platform for **generational wealth, food sovereignty, and cultural preservation,** rather than a disposable commodity sold to the highest bidder.

At their core, land trusts embody a radical reimagination of ownership: land is not just held, it is stewarded. It is kept for the many, not the few. It is honored as heritage, not exploited as profit. And in this stewardship lies a new definition of freedom: not just the right to walk the land, but the power to decide how it is used, preserved, and passed down.

Land trusts are the "Asue"-sou-sous of place, a collective covenant to secure what was nearly lost and to guarantee that no child of the diaspora grows up a stranger to their own soil.

The Bigger Picture

Universal Basic Income, cooperatives, rotating savings systems, and land trusts are not acts of charity. They are **strategic infrastructures for freedom**, deliberate designs that shift our communities from a state of reaction to one of resilience, from mere survival to true sovereignty.

Each model does something vital. **UBI** lays a foundation beneath families, ensuring that crises don't erase progress and that stability can seed a legacy. **Cooperatives** transform competition into collaboration, spreading risk and reward across many hands while circulating wealth where it belongs, within the community. **Rotating savings systems** remind us that trust is a form of currency, teaching discipline while multiplying opportunity, just as our ancestors did with sou-sous, partner hands, and tontines. And **land trusts** anchor us to the soil itself, securing place and heritage against the relentless tide of dispossession.

Together, these models dismantle the myth that freedom can be won through wages alone. They **convert individual hustle into collective power,** transforming short-term earnings into long-term assets, and ensuring that wealth does not evaporate at the end of each generation but compounds across time.

For too long, Black labor has been extracted without return, our brilliance fueling economies that left us empty-handed. These practices reclaim wealth, root it in community, and pass it forward. They remind us that liberation is not built on permission but on **possession**, not on access granted, but on ownership secured.

This is the blueprint: not a dream deferred, but a strategy deployed. When we build these systems together, we create legacies that last. Legacies that cannot be auctioned, erased, or outsourced. Legacies that declare: ***our survival was never the endgame, our sovereignty is.***

Legacy-Building vs. Survival Mode

Survival mode keeps us alive. Legacy-building sets us free. One merely sustains the body; the other secures the future. Survival is reactive, it responds to crises, hunger, and scarcity. Legacy is proactive, it builds empires, institutions, and endures as an inheritance. To shift from one to the other is to step out of the cycle of "just enough" and begin designing a cycle of "more than enough."

Survival mode is trauma's child. It is the reflex of a people denied security for generations, a conditioned response to centuries of stolen wealth and disrupted stability. In Black communities, survival often means juggling multiple jobs while still walking in poverty. It is the mother working two shifts and still unable to build savings, the father hustling on side gigs with no retirement plan, and the young graduate burdened with debt and unable to invest in a home. Studies show that 40% of U.S. Black households live in asset poverty meaning even with income, they lack the reserves to withstand a financial shock. This reality breeds exhaustion: paycheck-to-paycheck living, gig economies that consume hours without creating lasting equity, and endless hustle with no tangible harvest.

Legacy-building flips the script. It asks: ***What can I plant today that my children's children will eat from tomorrow?*** It moves beyond rent payments and into mortgages, beyond wages and into dividends, beyond labor and into ownership. Legacy demands we stop being consumers of other people's empires and start constructing our own.

Investing in education, building businesses, forming trusts, and securing land become multipliers where one generation's sacrifice seeds the next generation's innovation. In the Carolinas, Black legacy funds are now channeling resources into startups, cultural preservation, and land trusts, shifting communities away from gig survival and toward wealth creation. In the Caribbean, cooperative savings circles and community

Land trusts serve as vehicles of permanence, demonstrating that wealth can be anchored even in small island economies where foreign ownership is prevalent.

Legacy is not only financial, it is cultural, spiritual, and visionary. It is the wisdom of elders recorded in oral histories, the preservation of family land, the continuity of rituals, and the courage to imagine futures beyond oppression. Legacy is the proof that we are not merely surviving time; we are shaping it.

Survival mode says, "I must make it to tomorrow." Legacy-building declares, "I will build for the next hundred years."

Survival vs. Legacy in the Caribbean

The Caribbean shows the contrast in sharp relief. In Jamaica, survival mode appears to be a generation of young people struggling with 25% youth unemployment, often forced into underpaid jobs in the tourism industry or into migration. For many, survival means hustling daily with no guarantee of upward mobility, living one paycheck, one remittance, one crisis away from collapse.

Yet even here, the seeds of legacy sprout. In the diaspora, remittances flow like lifelines, funding schools, farms, housing projects, and family-owned businesses. These are not mere handouts; they are investments in permanence, transforming fleeting wages abroad into enduring assets at home. In Haiti, survival means navigating relentless instability political upheaval, scarcity, and disaster. But legacy shines through when remittances secure land, when diaspora families send capital that anchors roots in soil too often threatened with loss. Across Trinidad, Barbados, and Guyana, co-ops and credit unions turn survival savings into collective legacies, allowing ordinary people to resist the dominance of foreign corporations that control land, markets, and capital.

But here's the deeper truth: **survival mode is not destiny; it is a condition.** And conditions can change. They shift when people refuse to normalize scarcity as inevitable, when nations refuse to settle for permanent dependency. The pivot requires both **mindset** and **systems.**

- **Mindset:** A radical reshaping of financial literacy, discipline, and culture. It means teaching that wealth is not selfishness, that sacrifice today can secure a better future tomorrow, and that long-term planning is as heroic as the hustle.
- **Systems:** Policy advocacy for reparations, fair lending, community banking, and structural reforms that dismantle barriers to wealth. It is not enough for individuals to change habits; the architecture of inequality must be torn down and rebuilt.

Together, these shifts carve a path from survival to sovereignty. Legacy is not born overnight, it is built brick by brick, remittance by remittance, cooperative by cooperative. And once built, it resists erasure, declaring to the world that Black and Caribbean communities will no longer settle for survival alone. We are architects of permanence.

A New Cry: From Survival to Sovereignty

I don't believe freedom is just about being unchained. Real freedom is not simply the absence of oppression; it is the presence of ownership. Ownership of land. Ownership of businesses. Ownership of our time, our creativity, our resources, and our futures. Ownership that extends beyond the span of one life, anchoring generations in permanence and dignity.

This is the kind of freedom Black people in the South and across the Caribbean have too long been denied. From the rice fields of the Carolinas to the sugar estates of Jamaica and the Bahamas, we were forced to labor on land we could never claim, building wealth for empires that left us dispossessed. Even after emancipation, promises of land were betrayed, titles stolen, and access blocked by laws designed to keep us renters, not owners. Survival was permitted. Sovereignty was not.

But now, the cry rises again. From "40 acres and a mule" promised and stolen to ownership demanded and claimed, we lift our voices with fresh clarity: freedom is not employment it is enterprise. It is not simply the right to labor, it is the right to build, to keep, and to pass down.

In the Carolinas, it means protecting heirs' property from developers and turning family land into a lasting legacy. In Jamaica and Trinidad, it refers to cooperative farming, tech startups, and music industries owned by the people who create their own wealth. In The Bahamas, it means reclaiming coastlines and safeguarding family islands from foreign domination. In Haiti, it means transforming land insecurity into collective stewardship that no government can erase.

This is the new cry: **move beyond merely surviving the grind to building lasting legacies.**

To plant wealth where generations will harvest. To

own freedoms that will outlast us.

To transform survival into sovereignty, and labor into liberation.

Chapter 14

SMUGGLING US OUT OF POVERTY, A NEW UNDERGROUD RAILROAD

Harriet Tubman's words cut across centuries like a blade. They remind us that bondage is not always marked by iron shackles or auction blocks. Sometimes enslavement wears the disguise of normalcy. Sometimes it is the invisible weight of poverty, the endless grind that blinds us to the cage we inhabit.

Today, millions live chained not by law but by limitation convinced that endless struggle is inevitable, that hustling from "can't see to can't see" is the measure of life, and that survival itself is success. But survival is not freedom. Poverty is captivity. And until we recognize the trap, we cannot walk out of it.

That path, for our generation, must be a new Underground Railroad. Not trains or tunnels, but strategies and systems that smuggle us out of lack and into liberation. Just as Tubman built networks of safe houses, allies, and maps etched into memory, we must build networks of cooperative banks, land trusts, digital platforms, and wealth circles that move our people from dependency to dignity.

This Railroad is not about escaping into a single destination; it is about building routes to sovereignty wherever we are. In the Carolinas, it may appear as a combination of heirs' property protections and entrepreneurship hubs. In Jamaica, St. Vincent, St. Lucia, and The Bahamas, it may be cooperatives and community-owned resorts that keep wealth on our shores. In Haiti, it may mean farmer collectives and diaspora investments that bypass corrupt systems.

The lesson is clear: freedom requires routes. Freedom requires guides. Freedom requires courage to leave behind the known even when the known struggle, and step into the possibility of abundance.

This is the work of our time: to build a Railroad not of wood and iron, but of vision and structure. A Railroad that does not just smuggle bodies into safety, but ushers entire generations into sovereignty.

Just as Tubman once whispered truths in the dark, guiding the weary by moonlight, we need a modern Underground Railroad, an escape route not from plantations, but from poverty. This new railroad does not follow a North Star in the sky but a constellation of principles, systems, and networks that illuminate the way forward. Tubman's courage was not only in her flight to freedom but in her return, going back again to bring others out. That same spirit must fuel us now: to risk comfort for the sake of community, to pull others into the light, and to build a freedom that multiplies.

The Caribbean reminds us that resistance was never just running away, it was building anew. The Maroons carved entire worlds into hostile terrain, from Jamaica's Blue Mountains to the Surinamese rainforest. They did not merely survive, they designed sovereignty. They developed their own economies, guarded their own territories, and raised generations free from the slaveholder's gaze. They proved that liberation demands both courage to flee and creativity to be found.

In the U.S. South, the Great Dismal Swamp became another sanctuary, where thousands of freedom seekers built self-sustaining communities in the shadows of empire. Though less visible than their Caribbean counterparts, these swamp Maroons echoed the same lesson: freedom is not given, it is made. It is crafted in the cracks of oppression, defended with vigilance, and handed down through ingenuity.

Today, we inherited that blueprint. The new maroon societies will not be hidden in forests, but will be rooted in financial cooperatives, digital networks, land trusts, and cultural sovereignty. The new Railroad will not move along wooded paths but through systems of solidarity that allow us to carry each other across the thresholds of poverty into permanence. Like Tubman, like the Maroons, we are called not only to escape but to construct, to build economies, communities, and legacies that cannot be easily uprooted.

Today, these histories serve as blueprints for future endeavors. Just as the Maroons transformed wilderness into refuge, we must transform broken systems into platforms for independence. The old escapes were physical; the new escapes are economic. Where they carved free villages, we must carve free economies. Where they resist capture, we must resist exploitation. Where they build legacies in secrecy, we must build legacies in strategy.

In this chapter, we reimagine Tubman's blueprint for today. The whispers that once guided weary feet now become the whispers of financial literacy, shared in kitchens, barbershops, and churches, equipping families to navigate hostile systems with wisdom. The safe houses that once sheltered fugitives now take the form of community credit unions, cooperatives, and land trusts, fortresses of collective ownership where wealth circulates instead of leaking away. The coded songs and lanterns that once signaled the path to freedom now appear as digital platforms, mentorship networks, and rotating savings systems, modern signals of hope and strategy that cross borders as quickly as Wi-Fi.

Each one helping one. Each one teaches one. Each one lifting one. That is how we smuggle our people out of poverty, not through miracles, but through networks. The new Underground Railroad is not hidden; it is being built in plain sight. And its stations are not barns and swamps, but classrooms, community centers, and co-ops. It is a movement both quiet and loud, both spiritual and practical, both ancestral and futuristic.

Because liberation is not a solo act, it is a relay, one generation handing the torch of ownership, wisdom, and vision to the next.

In the Carolinas, the hidden histories of Black farmers and entrepreneurs remind us that independence once meant gripping the soil with both hands, holding land against all odds as the foundation of freedom. In the Caribbean, where poverty is often disguised beneath the glossy surface of tourism, resilience has long been forged through collective survival: Jamaican partner plans, Bahamian ***asue*** savings circles, Haitian ***konbit*** labor collectives. These were our old railroads of survival, improvised, communal, and often hidden from hostile eyes.

But survival alone is not enough. What once kept us afloat must now be transformed into what allows us to build. We cannot only whisper strategies in kitchens, we must codify them into institutions. We cannot only gather funds in secret, we must formalize them into credit unions, cooperatives, and trusts. We cannot only resist being uprooted, we must secure titles, craft policies, and create legal shields that ensure permanence. The time has come to modernize our railroads of survival into railroads of wealth, transforming secrecy into strategy and survival into sovereignty.

This new Underground Railroad is not about fleeing north; it is about rising where we stand. It is about reclaiming ownership of land, building businesses that feed our communities first, preserving heritage that cannot be bought out, and creating infrastructures of independence that no outside hand can dismantle.

Because freedom is not just unchained wrists, it is unlocked futures. It is the ability to rest without fear, to dream without limit, to plan without interruption, and to pass something forward without loss. True liberation means leading our people out of the darkness of survival and into the light of abundance, together, as builders, owners, and architects of our own destiny.

Inspired by Harriet Tubman's Methods: Whispering in Darkness, Moving in Silence, Going Back

Harriet Tubman's Underground Railroad was never a train. It was a network of courage, woven from whispers, shadows, and risk. Every escape demanded more than cunning; it demanded return trips into danger, an unrelenting commitment to free not just herself but as many as she could carry. Tubman's methods remain timeless, offering a blueprint for today's struggle, not for escaping plantations, but for escaping poverty, dependency, and systemic exploitation. The principles remain the same, but their expressions are new:

Whispering in Darkness. Tubman spread freedom through quiet truths whispered under the cover of night. Today, whispering means financial literacy passed in kitchens, community halls, and church basements. It means teaching our children the language of ownership, investment, and credit before the world teaches them debt and dependency. It means arming our people with knowledge that moves silently, invisibly, until it bursts forth as collective power.

Moving in Silence. Tubman understood that liberation required stealth, moving beneath the radar, evading the systems designed to ensnare. For us, this means building cooperatives, land trusts, and savings networks that operate outside exploitative institutions. It means refusing the visibility that invites premature destruction and instead cultivating resilience quietly, until it is unshakable. Moving in silence is not about hiding, it is about protecting fragile seeds until they grow strong enough to withstand the storm.

Going Back. Tubman's greatest defiance was not her escape, but her return, again, risking capture to bring others out. This is the principle we must recover: freedom is incomplete if it is not shared. Going back means mentoring, reinvesting, and lifting others as we rise. It means successful entrepreneurs creating pathways for those to come. It means diaspora wealth flowing home, not just outward. It means refusing the temptation of individual escape and instead building collective deliverance.

Tubman's genius was never just in flight; it was in blueprint. She demonstrated that freedom is not a one-way journey, but a cycle: whisper the truth, move with wisdom, and return for others. That is how she shattered chains in the 19th century, and it is how we must shatter poverty in the 21st.

Tubman whispered possibilities to the enslaved, planting seeds of hope in secret meetings, reminding them that freedom was not a myth but a path. Every whisper carried risk, but it also carried life, lighting sparks in the dark that could not be extinguished.

In our age, whispering in darkness is education. It is the quiet but revolutionary act of revealing truths hidden by systems of debt, exploitation, and manufactured ignorance. These whispers are the counter-script to centuries of lies that told us survival was the ceiling and ownership the privilege of others.

In the Carolinas, whispers rise in financial literacy workshops, neighbors teaching neighbors how to resist payday lenders, how to repair credit, how to escape the traps of redlining and wage theft. In Jamaica, whispers echo in church halls and youth programs where entrepreneurship is taught not as hustle, but as resistance, a way to create value without begging permission. In Haiti, grassroots groups whisper in Creole to peasants and street vendors, arming them with knowledge of cooperatives, land rights, and collective bargaining, transforming isolation into solidarity.

Whispering is not a weakness. It is a strategy. It is how revolutions begin, small truths passed hand to hand, ear to ear, until the murmur becomes a roar. Whispering is the seed stage of liberation: quiet enough to evade capture, powerful enough to take root in the imagination. For when people begin to hear that survival is not the limit, when they start to believe that legacy is possible, they are already walking toward freedom.

Moving in Silence

Tubman evaded patrols with coded songs, secret signals, and safe houses. Silence was her shield, her strategy, her survival. Every quiet step was a declaration that not all resistance needed to be announced, some of it was meant to be executed, lived, and passed down.

Today, moving in silence means creating discreet but powerful networks that operate outside the surveillance of exploitative systems. It is the art of building futures without broadcasting them to gatekeepers who would seek to deny or devour them.

In Jamaica, informal partner plans, such as sou-sou savings circles, continue to thrive, enabling participants to purchase homes, send their children to school, and launch businesses without needing to seek permission from a bank. In The Bahamas, quiet mentorship groups prepare young entrepreneurs to avoid predatory foreign contracts, teaching them how to negotiate ownership rather than servitude. In Trinidad and Guyana, women-led savings associations recycle wealth within communities, building financial resilience below the radar of colonial-style banking institutions.

Silence, here, is not weakness. It is wisdom. It is the choice to move deliberately, to protect vision until it is strong enough to withstand scrutiny, and to let results speak louder than announcements. The underground economies of the diaspora, such as rotating savings, community credit unions, and informal trade networks, are not accidental. They are the living legacy of Tubman's silence: networks that sustain, empower, and multiply without ever asking the system's permission.

Moving in silence does not mean hiding forever. It means nurturing in private what will one day transform the public. It means guarding seeds until the harvest is undeniable. And it means remembering that some of our greatest victories are prepared in whispers and grown in shadows until the time comes to step into the light.

Going Back

This was Tubman's hallmark. Nineteen times she returned south, liberating more than 300 souls, even with bounties on her head and death a constant shadow. Freedom for her was never solitary, it was multiplied. She refused to define liberation as her own escape. Instead, she described it as a responsibility: to carry others into light, no matter the cost.

Today, going back is the calling of those who break through barriers, refusing to shut the door behind them. It is not charity, it is a covenant. It is understood that individual success without collective uplift is incomplete; our victories are hollow if they are not shared.

We see this covenant alive in the Spelman and Morehouse-based Center for Black Entrepreneurship, where resources flow into training Carolina's startups, ensuring young founders do not face the struggle alone. We see this in the Afro-Caribbean Business Network in Canada, which connects diaspora capital back to Jamaica, Barbados, and Haiti, stitching together a transnational economy of return. We see it in Bahamian entrepreneurs who come home, not to flaunt success abroad, but to mentor youth, model ownership, and plant seeds of self-determination.

Going back means that one generation's achievement becomes the foundation for the next. It means refusing to let poverty recycle through the same neighborhoods while wealth migrates elsewhere. It means every degree, every dollar, every connection earned is repurposed into ladders for those still climbing.

Harriet Tubman showed us that freedom requires risk, trust, and relentless return. She smuggled people out of slavery. We must smuggle our people out of poverty. Whispering truths against lies. Building silent networks beneath oppressive systems. And always, always, going back for those still bound.

Liberation will not arrive through noise alone. It will come through strategy, solidarity, and the courage to carry more than ourselves into the light.

A New Cry: From Survival to Sovereignty

"Each one help one" is not a slogan, it is a survival strategy, liberation code, and economic blueprint. It is the modern echo of Tubman's collective escape, where freedom was never taken for one but always multiplied for many. Tubman risked everything because she understood that her liberation was incomplete if others remained bound. That same truth remains true today: individual success means little unless it leads to communal uplift.

This principle flows from African communal traditions and diasporic resilience. In the Carolinas, Black Connects national network pairs entrepreneurs with mentors, creating chains of opportunity: one business owner funded becomes an investor in the next. In Jamaica, Tropicana Community's ***Together We Can*** program equips high-risk teens with entrepreneurial skills, enabling them to "help one" within their circles and break cycles before they begin. In The Bahamas, the unwritten law of "each one teach one" thrives in cooperatives, where farmers share sustainable practices that raise incomes and secure food resilience. In Haiti, peasant collectives embody the principle that one successful harvest provides seeds and tools for the next, anchoring families against collapse.

It transforms isolated victories into communal triumphs. It ensures that no success story stands alone but becomes a foundation stone for the next. It is the difference between survival and sovereignty, between temporary relief and permanent power. It is how we modernize Tubman's Underground Railroad, not in secret paths through swamps and forests, but in visible networks of shared knowledge, pooled resources, and collective advance.

History as Blueprint: Susie King Taylor

History provides us with a model in Susie King Taylor, whose life embodied the phrase "each one help one" long before it gained widespread recognition. Born enslaved in Georgia, she risked everything to learn in secret schools and then risked even more to teach others, knowing that literacy was liberation. During the Civil War, she became the first Black Army nurse, tending to wound soldiers while also teaching them to read and write between battles. Her philosophy was radical in its simplicity: freedom that is hoarded is fragile; freedom that is shared becomes unbreakable. Every life she touched became a multiplier. Every student she taught was a seed for future liberation.

Susie King Taylor's legacy is evident liberation is not an individual endeavor. It is communal. Her life testified to a truth we must reclaim: the survival of the community rests on the willingness of one to uplift another.

Modern Echoes

Today, this ethos is not charity, it is strategy, it is investment, it is the architecture of freedom. When one entrepreneur mentors another, when one farmer shares tools with a neighbor, when one graduate funds the next student's education, freedom multiplies. Instead of competing in scarcity, we collaborate in abundance.

The North Star Black Cooperative Fellowship shows this in action: fellows trained in cooperative economics go on to mentor others, creating ripples that expand far beyond a single business or co-op. Across the Caribbean and the Carolinas, this principle is evident in mentorship networks, cooperative farming, and diaspora investment circles, each demonstrating that it is not just a sentiment but a survival strategy, not a slogan but a system.

This is Tubman's legacy extended. This is Taylor's philosophy lived out. Each helped one become a helper. Each uplifted soul becomes a rescuer. Liberation is not linear, it multiplies. Freedom spreads not by accident but by design, as those who escape poverty, ignorance, or exploitation turn back to open the path for others.

Together, we weave networks strong enough to smuggle us all from poverty's shadows into the dawn of true liberation. These networks are not abstract, they are cooperatives, land trusts, credit unions, and mentorship circles. They are the whispered truths passed in classrooms and kitchens, the silent strategies that bypass exploitative systems, the going back that ensures no victory is wasted.

True freedom is not the survival of the few but the sovereignty of the many. Tubman lit the way. Taylor multiplied the light. Now, it is ours to carry forward, each one helping one until shadows break into morning.

Escape has always required tools. For Harriet Tubman, there were maps whispered in song, safe houses lit by lanterns, and trusted guides who risked capture to lead others into freedom. Today, the chains are economic, but the principle is the same: liberation demands infrastructure. Our escape from poverty requires different tools networks such as our maps, mentorship as our guides, credit as our fuel, and connections as our safe houses. Together, they form the blueprint for an underground economy where Black communities can outmaneuver exploitation and chart their own paths to sovereignty.

Networks provide directions. In the Carolinas, platforms like Black Rise are more than business directories, they are modern maps, connecting entrepreneurs to capital, contracts, and each other. Every connection keeps wealth circulating within the community, rather than leaking outward. Across the Caribbean, cooperatives carry the same spirit. Jamaica's 200+ agricultural co-ops have increased member incomes by 25%, proving that collective organization multiplies effort and shields families from the vulnerabilities of isolation.

Mentorship becomes guidance. Just as Tubman returned again to lead others out, those who have walked the road of business, ownership, and education must turn back to guide the next. In Barbados, mentorship hubs for young entrepreneurs connect elders with rising innovators, passing not just advice but also strategies that can save years of struggle. In the U.S. South, HBCU incubators are modern "conductors," equipping students to build legacies rather than chase jobs.

Credit fuels movement. Where Tubman needed supplies and allies, we need access to fair lending and investment. Too often, predatory credit systems shackle Black families in debt, while mainstream finance denies loans. Community credit unions and rotating savings systems flip the script: they are not handouts, but engines, fueling homes, startups, and education without exploitation.

Connection creates refuge. Tubman relied on safe houses. Today, our safe houses are community spaces, co-working hubs, cultural centers, digital platforms, that offer protection, resources, and trust. They are sanctuaries where ideas are nurtured and futures secured.

The lesson is clear: freedom is not won alone. Just as the Underground Railroad relied on collaboration, our escape from poverty requires collective tools. Networks, mentorship, credit, and connection are not luxuries, they are lifelines.

Mentorship Lights the Way, Credit Unlocks the Doors

Mentorship has always been a lantern in the dark. Tubman guided the weary step by step, whispering courage when fear threatened to consume them. Today, mentorship carries that same power, not just to encourage, but to illuminate pathways otherwise hidden. Programs like **Accelerating Business Leadership and Entrepreneurship (ABLE)** pair African diaspora founders with seasoned experts, raising their chances of long-term success by nearly 30%. Each mentor becomes a modern conductor, charting safe passage through the obstacles of capital, contracts, and scaling. In the Caribbean, mentorship thrives in youth programs across Trinidad, Guyana, and Jamaica, where entrepreneurial training equips young people to reject dependency and instead **build enterprises that last beyond their lifetime.** Mentorship is not charity, it is a chain of light, passed from one generation to the next, ensuring no one walks blind.

Credit, too, is liberation's engine. Without fuel, even the bravest journeys come to a halt. For generations, banks denied Black borrowers' fair access to capital, forcing communities to invent their own financial engines. In The Bahamas, **sou-sou savings circles** continue to fund startups, weddings, and homes, relying on community-based systems rather than predatory banking practices. In Jamaica, these informal networks have evolved into structured partnership plans and credit unions, offering low-interest loans that stabilize households and support business growth. In Haiti, farmer cooperatives pool resources to buy equipment, resisting dependency on foreign lenders. Here, credit is not just cash, it is **collective trust converted into capital.**

When mentorship lights the way and credit fuels the journey, escape becomes possible. Together, they turn impossible dreams into concrete legacies.

Connections bridge gaps. The Underground Railroad thrived not only because brave individuals acted, but also because safe houses were linked together in a living web of trust, secrecy, and solidarity. No single lantern in a window was enough on its own; freedom required a chain of lights stretching across hostile terrain. Today, those same principles apply. Our modern escape from poverty and dispossession demands connection ties that link isolated efforts into collective power.

Cross-border partnerships serve as those modern safe houses. The Afro Caribbean Business Network builds bridges between the diaspora and the islands, connecting Carolina-based mentors with Bahamian, Jamaican, and Barbadian innovators to forge joint ventures that keep wealth circulating within the Black world. These connections transform isolation into infrastructure, turning scattered sparks into a system of fire. They remind us that liberation is not only a local fight, it is a global one.

When networks, mentorship, credit, and connections are woven together, they form the new escape routes of our time. We see their impact everywhere: in U.S. Black cooperatives generating over $500 million annually; in churches that quietly serve as savings circles, where dollars become engines of trust; and in HBCUs like Spelman and Morehouse, where incubators turn raw vision into viable ventures. These are not just programs,they are lifelines, carrying our people step by step out of the shadows of scarcity into the dawn of self-determination.

The charge, then, is clear: the Black elite, the institutions, the "seen" must extend their hands back to the "unseen." Just as Tubman risked everything to return for those still bound, we too must refuse to mistake our own advancement for collective liberation. To escape alone is survival; to bring others with us is revolution.

"We can free thousands more, if only they knew they were still enslaved by poverty."

Like Tubman's unseen railroad, this modern one operates in whispers and returns, each one helping one, networks guiding the way. In the Carolinas and the Caribbean, we must build it: **owning our escape, freeing souls from economic bondage, and ensuring no one is left in the fields.** Freedom isn't merely unchained it is owned, passed down, and multiplied.

Chapter 15

STILL CAN'T SEE, BUT NOW WE KNOW WHERE TO LOOK

Even in the thick fog of "can't see," when the horizon feels swallowed in darkness and the grind blinds our vision, there are always glimmers. Faint, steady lights piercing through signals not of fantasy, but of possibility. They do not point to a distant, unreachable land of freedom. They point to practical, proven paths we have overlooked for too long.

The truth is this: survival has trained our eyes on the ground, on the immediate, on the daily hustle that feeds today but starves tomorrow. But now, we know where to look. Not to luck. Not to promises from governments or corporations that have betrayed us in the past. We look instead to communities who have cracked the code who have structured survival into sovereignty, who have turned scarcity into systems, who have built resilience strong enough to stand against storms that were designed to destroy them.

From the Carolinas' resilient shores to the Caribbean's unyielding islands, where poverty's fog still lingers like humidity in the air, the lessons are everywhere if we dare to notice. Freedom is not a windfall. It is not a charitable gift wrapped up and handed down. Freedom is a design. It is built like an institution, brick by brick, system by system, until what was once fragile becomes fortified.

We see it in Jewish communities, who once scattered and scarred by exile, pogroms, and genocide, built vast networks of mutual aid, communal credit unions, and intergenerational banking systems. These transformed displacement into diaspora strength, ensuring that wherever they landed, they had the capital to build again.

We see it in Asian immigrant communities, often barred from mainstream financing or treated as perpetual outsiders, who created rotating credit associations, family investment pools, and cooperative lending systems. These models, built on trust rather than access to Wall Street, transformed corner shops into corporate empires and laundromats into lasting legacies.

These are not secrets to guard like treasure. They are blueprints waiting to be adapted, reimagined, and expanded. Their strength was never found in individual hustle alone, it was found in collective infrastructure. And if others could build in exile, in exclusion, and in oppression, then so can we.

For us, the lesson is clear: this is not about envy, it is about evolution. We are not here to imitate another people's blueprint, but to sharpen our own. We must shift from "I made it" to "we rise together." For what good is one seed if the soil remains barren? The true measure of liberation is not one person breaking through while the rest remain trapped; it is a community climbing together, hand in hand, refusing to leave anyone behind.

Freedom must be redefined. It is not a lottery ticket for the lucky few. It is not a fragile heritage that slips through fingers in one generation. No freedom is a deliberate structure, a house built on stone, crafted through networks, cooperatives, trusts, and legacies that endure storms and outlast lifetimes.

And so, in this final chapter, I call us higher. Higher than survival. Higher than the grind. Higher than individual success that dies in silence. I call us to collective responsibility, to the discipline of building systems so strongly that even if our names are forgotten, the structures will remain. Let us rise beyond the grind and claim a vision broad enough for generations unborn.

This is our rallying cry:
To move from 'can't see to can see'. From
merely surviving to truly building.
From endlessly grinding to endlessly growing.

We are no longer lost in the dark. The fog is lifting. The lights are above us. And now we know where to look and more importantly, we know how to build. Together, we will.

Lessons from Other Communities (Jewish, Asian, Chinese) That Protect, Pool, and Reinvest

No community thrives in isolation. Success is never random, it is structured, safeguarded, and handed down. Across history, Jewish, Asian, and Chinese diaspora communities have turned exile, exclusion, and discrimination into laboratories of resilience. They survived not because the world welcomed them, but because they built internal systems of survival, anchored in protection, pooling, and reinvestment.

Jewish communities, scattered by persecution, developed **Gamach** (free-loan societies) and mutual aid networks where every dollar circulated inward before it ever leaked outward. Asian immigrants in America, denied access to banks, built **rotating credit associations** that turned corner shops into dynasties and children into corporate heirs. Chinese diasporas worldwide have practiced **"guanxi" networks** webs of trust, obligation, and reciprocity that make individual success impossible to separate from communal progress.

These models were never about charity. They were about **discipline.** About refusing to let capital, skills, or opportunity escape the hands of the community until it had multiplied. They remind us that wealth is not built on individual hustle alone but on collective infrastructure, on structures designed to catch each member before they fall and to lift each one higher when they rise.

For the Black South and the Caribbean, these are not foreign strategies; they are **adaptable blueprints for success.** Protection means shielding family land from predatory development. Pooling means reviving sou-sou, partner, and credit unions as engines of capital. Reinvestment means refusing to let wealth exist after one generation; instead, it turns it into legacies of land, businesses, and education.

These communities reveal a truth we cannot ignore freedom without infrastructure is unsustainable. Liberation requires not just escape, but structure. Not just resistance, but reinvestment. And if others could turn oppression into strategy, then so can we.

The Jewish Model: Protection as Justice

The Jewish community exemplifies protection through deeply rooted safety nets that ensure no family is left to collapse. After centuries of persecution and displacement, and especially in the wake of the Holocaust, survival became a structure. Organizations such as the Jewish Federations of North America raise billions of dollars **annually,** channeling those funds into education, healthcare, small business development, and rapid crisis response. Their ethic of **tzedakah** charity reframed not as generosity but as **justice owed** redefined giving as an obligation to the community's survival.

Through this model, capital is never idle. Interest-free loans circulate through families and neighborhoods, funding college degrees, launching businesses, and stabilizing households until they can stand on their own. Over time, this system has not only met needs but also multiplied wealth. Jewish households today hold **three to four times the median wealth of U.S. households,** not solely due to chance or privilege, but because of an infrastructure deliberately built to **carry every generation forward.**

For the Carolinas and the Caribbean, the lesson is urgent: protection is power. Black communities can mirror this blueprint by establishing **land trusts** that shield Gullah-Geechee properties from predatory gentrification, by building solidarity funds that buy back ancestral lands piece by piece, and by reinvesting not just in survival, but in **enterprises that foster memory and identity, such as** eco-tourism ventures, cultural preservation businesses, and heritage cooperatives. These are not just economic plays; they are declarations that our history, our land, and our legacy will not be erased.

Protection, when designed as justice, is not passive. It is aggressive preservation. It is the wall against erasure, the shield against exploitation, and the foundation upon which wealth can be safely passed.

Pooling: Turning Small Contributions into Big Capital

Asian immigrant communities have long demonstrated the power of collective pooling, proving that what seems small when isolated becomes transformative when combined. Systems like the Chinese **hui** or the Korean **kye** operate on trust, discipline, and reciprocity. Every member contributes to a common pot, and each cycle, one member receives the lump sum to invest in a business, purchase property, or cover a major expense. These networks, built without the approval of banks that historically excluded them, became parallel financial systems that fueled community growth.

The results are undeniable. In the U.S., more than **50% of Korean Americans own small businesses,** many of them financed through these rotating credit associations. Chinatowns in New York, San Francisco, and Toronto did not grow because outside institutions granted them capital they thrived because communities **pooled their own resources first,** building grocery stores, laundries, and restaurants into vibrant economic ecosystems. Only once stability was established did outside capital begin to flow in.

Pooling is more than saving it is **sovereign investment.** It transforms scarcity into seed money, multiplying opportunity through trust. It teaches financial discipline, reinforces solidarity, and ensures that wealth circulates inside the community before it leaks out.

For the Caribbean and the Carolinas, the blueprint is already in place. Jamaica's **partner plans,** Trinidad's **sou-sou,** and Bahamian **asue circles** embody the same principle but they remain largely informal. Formalizing them into **cooperatives, credit unions, and community banks** could expand their scale and impact. Imagine if these funds didn't just buy homes or cars, but seeded **Black-owned hotels in Nassau, renewable energy projects in Jamaica, or shipping cooperatives across the Eastern Caribbean.** By structuring pooling into institutional power, we shift from survival finance to sovereignty finance.

Pooling, then, is not merely about rotating cash. It is about building economic ecosystems that insulate communities from exploitation, empower ownership, and turn "a little from many" into empires that endure.

Reinvestment: Closing the Loop of Wealth

Pooling is powerful but only if the profits are reinvested in the community. Without reinvestment, money leaks outward, enriching outsiders instead of building internal strength. This is the genius of Jewish and Asian diaspora models: every dollar earned is deliberately reinvested in schools, businesses, and assets that strengthen the next generation.

For Jewish communities, reinvestment has meant funding scholarships, synagogues, and cultural centers that preserve identity while building professional pipelines. For Asian immigrant enclaves, reinvestment is evident in Koreatowns and Chinatowns across the U.S. and Canada economic ecosystems where restaurants, markets, real estate offices, and banks all interconnect. A single dollar circulates 6–10 times before leaving the community, multiplying its impact and creating chains of ownership that span generations.

The numbers tell the story: despite facing discrimination, **Asian American households now hold median wealth nearly double the U.S. average.** This did not happen by chance. It happened because profits were not immediately consumed but reinvested in **education, real estate, and business ventures.** The community became its own venture capitalist.

For the Black diaspora, this principle is urgent. Reinvestment must become more than individual charity it must be collective policy. Imagine tourism profits in Jamaica funding tech hubs in Kingston, or remittances from Haitians abroad financing housing cooperatives in Port-au-Prince. Picture Bahamian agricultural or tourism earnings reinvested into renewable energy grids, or Carolina entrepreneurs channeling profits into local HBCU endowments and land trusts.

Reinvestment is not just an economic concept it is also a form of resistance. It transforms fleeting income into a legacy. It ensures that what we earn doesn't evaporate into outside systems but flows back like a river nourishing, expanding, and sustaining. For our people, reinvestment is the bridge between hustle and heritage, between fleeting gain and lasting freedom across generations.

The Chinese Government and Diaspora Support

A unique lesson comes from China. Unlike many nations that neglect or even resent their diaspora, the Chinese government recognized early on that its people abroad were not a liability, but a strategic asset. For decades, it actively cultivated this relationship through policies and infrastructure designed to transform overseas communities into partners in national development.

Through the ***qiaowu*** **system** a set of government programs focused on "overseas Chinese affairs" China established deliberate connections with its global diaspora. These included **tax incentives for returning capital, legal pathways for joint ventures, recognition ceremonies for diaspora donors, and even political influence** for those who invested in schools, hospitals, and infrastructure back home. Rather than leaving remittances to chance, China **organized them into a national strategy.**

The results were transformative. By the late 20th century, **billions in diaspora capital flowed into China's coastal provinces,** funding factories, highways, ports, and universities. Many of the iconic "Made in China" industries were seeded not by foreign corporations, but by overseas Chinese who returned with savings, skills, and connections. This symbiosis created a loop: diaspora capital built the homeland, and a rising homeland empowered its diaspora with renewed pride and opportunities for expansion.

The lesson for the Black diaspora is profound. Scattered from the Carolinas to Kingston, from London to Lagos, our remittances are already enormous **over $50 billion annually from the Caribbean and African diaspora alone.** However, these flows are often fragmented, confined to private family transfers, or diverted by Western banks and money transfer companies. Imagine if governments, churches, and institutions **aligned with community networks to coordinate this power** transforming remittances into collective investment funds, cooperative banks, and development trusts.

If China could build highways and factories from diaspora capital, why can't Black nations and communities build **land trusts, schools, cultural centers, renewable energy grids, and tech hubs?** If China can create policies that incentivize overseas reinvestment, why can't our governments craft laws that protect family land, lower barriers for diaspora entrepreneurs, and ensure our remittances circulate more effectively within **our own economies?**

The Chinese example proves that diaspora is not distance, it is power. When harnessed strategically, it becomes one of the greatest engines for national and collective wealth. The task before us is clear: to stop treating our diaspora as scattered individuals sending money to home and start organizing it as a **global nation without borders capable of building futures together.**

The Blueprint

The lesson across these communities is simple but profound: **freedom is not improvised, it is structured.** It is protected, pooled, reinvested, and coordinated until it outlasts generations. Each successful diaspora in history has demonstrated this pattern, and now it is our turn to adapt it to our struggle.

- **Protect** with solidarity funds, land trusts, and cooperative ownership structures that shield assets from loss and predatory capture. Just as Jewish federations ensured no family fell into despair, Black communities in the Carolinas and Caribbean must build buffers funds that buy back ancestral land, trusts that secure Gullah-Geechee and Bahamian family holdings, and safety nets that prevent generational collapse. Protection is preservation.
- **Pool** through rotating credit systems, cooperatives, and communal finance that multiply scarce resources into large-scale capital. Asian immigrant groups turned tiny contributions into thriving businesses and property empires. We already practice this in sou-sou circles, partners, and box hands. The call now is to formalize and expand them,creating cooperative banks, credit unions, and Black-led venture pools that fuel hotels, farms, tech startups, and renewable energy ventures across our diaspora. Pooling transforms survival into scalability.
- **Reinvest** in education, real estate, and enterprises that sustain generational wealth. Jewish and Asian households grew wealth not simply by earning, but by closing the loop, ensuring each dollar returned to their communities through schools, businesses, and housing. For us, reinvestment must mean funding HBCUs, financing Caribbean universities, developing diaspora-owned real estate, and seeding industries that employ our own. Reinvestment is regeneration.
- **Coordinate diaspora capital** with governments, churches, and community institutions, turning remittances into long-term assets. China's qiaowu system proved the power of aligning diaspora resources with national development. Black communities worldwide send billions home every year, yet too much of it evaporates into consumption. Imagine if we organized these flows into development funds, cooperative investment portfolios, and land trusts. Coordination turns scattered generosity into collective power.

For Black communities in the Carolinas, the Caribbean, and beyond, this is not about imitation, it is about **adaptation.** It is about refusing to remain fragmented and instead choosing to structure our freedom. Because freedom is never just unchained, it is owned, protected, multiplied, and passed forward.

This is the new blueprint. Not survival, but sovereignty. Not hustle, but heritage. Not grind, but generational vision.

Collective Responsibility: Not Just "I Made It," but "We Rise Together"

The myth of "I made it" isolates the survivor from the struggling, turning success into a lonely fortress surrounded by walls of scarcity. It suggests that freedom is personal, that wealth is private, and that survival is enough. But true liberation has never been about one person's escape, it is measured by how many we pull up behind us. Individual triumph without community transformation is not victory, it is a form of abandonment.

Collective responsibility demands a different ethic. It insists that our victories become ladders, that our wealth becomes bridges, and that our freedom becomes an inheritance. This is the power of "we rise together", an ethic strong enough to rebuild fractured communities, restore generational wealth, and reimagine survival into sovereignty.

This responsibility is not new. It is rooted in African communalism, in the timeless philosophy of **ubuntu:** "I am because we are." For centuries, this principle has guided survival under oppression, reminding us that no one stands alone. Even in the worst conditions, on plantations, in maroon villages, in refugee camps, the ethic of collective care ensured that children were fed, the sick were tended, and knowledge was passed down.

In the U.S., too many Black professionals who "make it" wrestle with survivor's guilt, knowing their success stands against a backdrop of systemic exclusion. But guilt must not paralyze. The question is not, ***"Why me?"*** but ***"Who can I carry with me?"***

We see this ethic alive in modern structures. The **National Black MBA Association** pairs executives with young professionals, creating pipelines of mentorship, scholarships, and seed funding that multiply impact. In the Carolinas, Black-owned incubators connect first-generation founders with networks of investors who were once denied those same opportunities. In Jamaica and Trinidad, alumni associations abroad send remittances not only to families but to schools, clinics, and co-ops,transforming private success into public investment.

Collective responsibility is not charity, it is strategy. It is how communities once denied capital build capital. It is how one victory becomes ten. It is how freedom stops being fragile and becomes fortified.

Because the truth is this: if our success does not ripple outward, it will dry up inward. But when one helps another, when each one teaches another, when every individual wins, it becomes communal wealth,then we rise, not as isolated survivors, but as a people unchained, unbroken, and unstoppable.

In the Carolinas, the principle is visible in action. Initiatives like **Charlotte's Black Entrepreneurship Week** unite established leaders with emerging startups, ensuring knowledge, resources, and contracts cycle back into the community. It is no longer about the lone pioneer breaking glass ceilings; it is about building skylines together.

The Caribbean echoes the same call. In Jamaica, the story of the "barrel children", raised by remittances from abroad, has turned full circle. As adults, many now return through organizations like the **Jamaican Diaspora Youth Connect,** bringing back skills in technology, agriculture, and business, determined to reverse the brain drain and plant seeds of innovation at home.

In The Bahamas, the tradition of "each one teaches one" should live on through scholarships funded by successful entrepreneurs who remember their roots and refuse to let the next generation drown in the tide of poverty. In Haiti, women's cooperatives should exemplify this model: profits should not be pocketed by a few, but pooled to send children to school, ensuring that individual gain blossoms into collective ascent.

Collective responsibility is not charity is survival evolved. It is a refusal to repeat cycles of isolation. It is a declaration that freedom achieved alone is freedom incomplete. By rejecting "I made it" isolation for "we rise" solidarity, we transform individual wins into communal revolutions. We honor ancestors who did not dream of solitary escape, but of elevation for all.

The measure of our generation will not be how many broke through barriers, it will be how many we pulled through with us.

Collective responsibility also reframes success itself. Achievement is no longer measured solely by income, titles, or proximity to power, but by circulation,how resources, knowledge, and access move through a community rather than stall at the top. Wealth that does not circulate hardens into isolation; success that does not multiply becomes brittle. A people rise not when one escapes scarcity, but when systems are built so escape is no longer necessary.

This ethic requires intentional design. It calls for cooperative ownership, shared equity models, and institutions that reward reinvestment over extraction. From community land trusts to credit unions, from worker-owned businesses to diaspora-backed venture funds, collective responsibility transforms individual progress into durable infrastructure. These are not sentimental gestures; they are strategic responses to histories that deliberately denied collective accumulation.

Ultimately, "we rise together" is not a slogan,it is a survival doctrine refined into vision. It insists that freedom must be scalable, transferable, and inheritable. When success becomes communal, it no longer evaporates with one person's fall or fatigue. It endures. And in that endurance, the long arc from "can't see to can't see" bends,not toward endless grind, but toward shared elevation and lasting sovereignty.

Collective responsibility also restores time as a shared asset. When individuals are forced to fight alone, time is consumed by survival. But when communities pool resources and support one another, time is freed for learning, planning, and creation. This is how generations recover stolen futures,not through isolated breakthroughs, but through shared breathing room that allows vision to outpace crisis.

It also redefines leadership. True leaders are not those who rise fastest, but those who widen the path behind them. Leadership rooted in collective responsibility invests in succession, not dominance; in teaching, not hoarding; in building institutions that outlast personalities. This model rejects the scarcity mindset imposed by oppression and replaces it with durability,the understanding that power grows when it is shared.

Yet collective responsibility is not without tension. It demands sacrifice, patience, and the willingness to resist individualism in a culture that celebrates personal escape. It asks those who have "made it" to remain accountable to places and people that may still be struggling. This is difficult work, but necessary work, because systems that fractured communities will not be undone by solitary success.

History confirms this truth. Every lasting gain,from mutual aid societies to civil rights victories, from cooperative economics to labor protections,was achieved collectively. These advances were never the product of lone heroes, but of coordinated effort, shared risk, and communal resolve. Progress, when it lasts, is always plural.

The task before us, then, is generational. Collective responsibility is how we turn survival into inheritance and endurance into power. It is how we ensure that freedom is not fragile, temporary, or dependent on individual fortune. When success becomes communal, the grind loses its grip, the future gains shape, and liberation moves from possibility to permanence.

FINAL CALL: FREEDOM IS NOT INHERITED, IT'S STRUCTURED

Freedom is not a gift that falls from the sky, nor a treasure passed down unearned. **Freedom is built**. It is a deliberate architecture of systems, policies, and mindsets, brick by brick, that ensures it endures beyond a single generation's grasp. Without structure, freedom evaporates; with structure, it multiplies.

This final call demands more than reflection demands action.

- **Structure through reparations.** In the Carolinas, advocate for land grants and restitution policies that mirror successful models elsewhere, Jewish Holocaust restitution funds, Native American tribal trusts, even the German government's payments to Jewish survivors. These precedents prove that repair is possible when there is will. Structured reparations would anchor Black inheritance not in dreams, but in deeds.

- **Structure through policy reform.** In the Caribbean, nations like Jamaica and The Bahamas must strive to reclaim and nationalize key tourism assets, transforming foreign-controlled resorts into revenue streams that support community funds, education, and local entrepreneurship. The same beaches that exploit workers today can finance their liberation tomorrow, if ownership shifts from foreign pockets to national hands.
- **Structure through education.** No freedom is sustainable without knowledge. Just as many Asian communities emphasize STEM and financial literacy as cultural imperatives, Black communities must weave ownership, economics, and cooperative models into school curricula. In Haiti, community-led reforms to secure land titles offer another critical form of education, teaching people the legal and practical skills to retain what is theirs, prevent land theft, and ensure intergenerational continuity.
- **Structure through economic innovation.** Freedom must be funded. Pilot programs in **Universal Basic Income (UBI),** government incentives for cooperatives, and targeted wealth taxes on elites can finance reinvestment in Black communities. These aren't handouts,they're structural reinforcements, scaffolding that ensures the house of freedom doesn't collapse under pressure.

Freedom structured is freedom sustained. This is how we ensure it is not fleeting but foundational.

And so, we close with our mandate:
From **can't see to can see.**
From **surviving to building.**
From **grinding to growing.**

These words are not a mantra, they are instructions. In the Carolinas and the Caribbean, we have learned from others' lessons, honored our ancestors' sacrifices, and committed ourselves to a collective rise. Now, the fog is lifting. We know where to look. We know what to build. And together, we will arrive, not inheriting chains, but handing down choices.

REFLECTION ON FROM CAN'T SEE TO CAN'T SEE

From ***Can't See to Can't See*** is not just a history of labor, poverty, and resilience it is a manifesto for liberation. The title itself evokes the relentless grind of Black labor, from dawn's first dim light to night's final shadows, where survival was prioritized over rest, ownership, or vision. Yet across its chapters, the book dismantles this narrative of endless toil, replacing it with strategies for rest, healing, ownership, and collective freedom.

The early chapters frame rest as a revolutionary act. Drawing from Tricia Hersey's ***Nap Ministry,*** the Sabbath tradition, and even cross-cultural wisdom from Judaism, Islam, Buddhism, and Confucianism, the book establishes that liberation begins with reclaiming time. Rest is not laziness; it is rebellion. It is a refusal to be defined by labor and an insistence that Black lives deserve rhythm, peace, and restoration. This spiritual and cultural grounding sets the stage for a more profound exploration of what true freedom entails.

The middle chapters turn to ownership as the cornerstone of liberation. The cry for "40 acres and a mule" is reframed as a modern demand for land, businesses, and generational control. Drawing from examples in the Carolinas, Jamaica, Haiti, and the Bahamas, the text illustrates how dispossession has been the consistent tool of oppression, whether through discriminatory lending, land grabs, or foreign exploitation of Caribbean economies. But the counterstrategy is clear: cooperative models, rotating savings systems like sou-sou, land trusts, and intentional reinvestment. Ownership, not employment, is the true pathway to sovereignty.

From there, the book brilliantly reimagines Harriet Tubman's Underground Railroad as a metaphor for smuggling people out of poverty. Just as Tubman risked everything to go back for more, modern leaders, mentors, and entrepreneurs must build networks of escape through credit, mentorship, cooperative economics, and principle. Here, the book honors figures like Susie King Taylor, blending her legacy of healing and teaching with Tubman's courage to highlight the power of communal uplift. These stories insist that freedom is not individual but collective.

The final chapters widen the lens to global lessons. Jewish communities' reinvestment models, Asian diaspora savings clubs, and even state-backed strategies, such as China's support of its diaspora, reveal that wealth is structured, not accidental. These blueprints reinforce the central claim of the book: freedom is not inherited, it is built, protected, and passed down through deliberate systems and institutions. Collective responsibility replaces the myth of "I made it," calling for a "we rise together" ethos across the diaspora.

Ultimately, ***From Can't See to Can't See*** is both a lament and a rallying cry. It laments centuries of toil without legacy, survival without sovereignty, and fatigue without rest. But it also declares a vision: from surviving to building, from struggling to thriving, from darkness to dawn. The book's greatest strength is its balance of historical depth, spiritual grounding, and practical strategy. It does not romanticize struggle; it offers blueprints for liberation.

In reflecting on its message, one is struck by the continuity of the cry for freedom. The ancestors who labored dreamed of more than survival. They dreamed of legacy. This book challenges us to honor that dream, not just with words, but with systems that ensure our children inherit not chains, but choices.

Our Dayenu A Song of Survival and Triumph

If he had carried our ancestors through the Middle Passage but not given them the will to survive
(It would have been enough!)

If He had given them the will to survive, but not the faith to sing in chains
(It would have been enough!)

If He had given them the faith to sing in chains, but not the courage to fight for freedom
(It would have been enough!)

If he had given them the courage to fight but not deliver emancipation
(It would have been enough!)

If he had delivered emancipation, but not raised up leaders for justice
(It would have been enough!)

If he had raised up leaders but not given us civil rights victories
(It would have been enough!)

If he had given us civil rights but not restored pride in our culture **(It would have been enough!)**

If he had restored our culture but not opened doors to education **(It would have been enough!)**

If he had opened doors to education, but not blessed us with family strength **(It would have been enough!)**

If He had blessed us with family, but not given us vision for wealth and independence **(It would have been enough!)**

If he had given us wealth and independence, but not kept us still rising
(It would have been enough!)

CLOSING

God, we thank you for all that you have done.
You have done enough more than enough.
And still, you are not finished with us.

WORKBOOK: FROM CAN'T SEE TO CAN'T SEE, QUESTIONS & REFLECTIONS

MULTIPLE-CHOICE QUESTIONS (15)

(Answers included in bold)

1. The phrase "from can't see to can't see" refers to:

   A) A migration path across the Atlantic

   B) A proverb about perseverance

   C) Working from before sunrise to after sunset

   D) The Underground Railroad

2. Harriet Tubman's leadership of the Underground Railroad is best described as:

   A) A single escape path through Maryland

   B) A political campaign for abolition

   C) A network of safe houses and allies enabling escape

   D) An armed rebellion

3. During slavery and its aftermath, women's "invisible labor" included:

   A) Farm ownership

   B) Domestic work, caregiving, and community survival tasks

   C) Political organizing

   D) Industrial management

4. What does the concept of "rest as resistance" emphasize?

   A) Sleep as a luxury for elites

   B) Napping as laziness

   C) Rest as a revolutionary act against exploitation

   D) Vacation as economic privilege

5. Which system is often used in Caribbean and African communities to build shared wealth?

   A) Stock exchanges

   B) Banking co-ops

   C) Susu (rotating savings groups)

   D) Microloans

6. In pandemics and crises, "essential yet expendable" refers to:

   A) Political leaders

   B) Workers who are vital but underpaid and unprotected

   C) Business owners

   D) Retirees

7. One risk of migration in Caribbean families is:
   A) Increased tourism
   B) Higher wages for everyone
   C) Separation of families and unequal burdens
   D) Access to more land

8. Civil rights victories often led to:
   A) Immediate equality in all sectors
   B) Abandonment of cultural identity
   C) Increased access to education and opportunity
   D) Disappearance of racism

9. Which phrase captures the meaning of "Dayenu"?
   A) Freedom delayed is freedom denied
   B) Keep pushing
   C) It would have been enough
   D) Justice now

10. Which of the following is an example of ownership creating liberation?
    A) Working extra shifts at a factory
    B) Owning farmland or a small business
    C) Becoming a political candidate
    D) Attending college only

11. Generational wealth is best defined as:
    A) Lottery winnings
    B) Assets and resources passed from one generation to the next
    C) Government stipends
    D) Temporary income boosts

12. Which was not a strategy for survival during slavery?

    A) Singing spirituals

    B) Creating support networks

    C) Political campaigning

    D) Building cultural pride

13. The phrase "Freedom is not inherited , it's structured" suggests:

    A) Freedom is automatic

    B) Freedom requires intentional systems and institutions

    C) Freedom is a gift from leaders

    D) Freedom can be ignored

14. Youth "brain drain" in the Caribbean refers to:

    A) Young people's resistance movements

    B) Migration of talented youth abroad due to a lack of opportunities

    C) Decline in literacy rates

    D) Shorter lifespans

15. Which labor pattern is most associated with post-slavery economies in the South and Caribbean?

    A) Wage equality

    B) Corporate contracts

    C) Sharecropping and plantation labor systems

    D) Entrepreneurial ownership

SHORT-ANSWER QUESTIONS (10)

1. What does "from can't see to can't see" reveal about the exploitation of labor historically?
2. How did Harriet Tubman's strategies create models for liberation beyond physical escape?
3. In what ways can invisible labor by women be recognized and valued today?
4. Why is rest considered a revolutionary act in communities burdened by overwork?
5. How does a Susu or rotating savings group work, and why has it endured?
6. Describe a modern example of workers being called "essential" but treated as expendable.
7. How has migration shaped the economic stories of Caribbean families you know?
8. Why is ownership often viewed as more liberating than wage labor?
9. What does "freedom must be structured" mean in today's context?
10. How can youth talent be retained and nurt***ured in Caribbean nations?***

ESSAY QUESTIONS (5)

1. Compare the labor conditions of enslaved Africans working "from can't see to can't see" with modern forms of overwork and economic exploitation. How do these parallels affect our understanding of freedom today?

2. Harriet Tubman used networks of trust, strategy, and community to lead people to freedom. What would a modern "economic underground railroad" look like, and who might it serve?

3. Discuss the role of women's invisible labor in sustaining families and communities historically. How can recognizing this labor reshape gender equity today?

4. Examine the tension between jobs and ownership in Black communities. Why has ownership been a path to liberation, and what barriers still exist?

5. "Freedom is not inherited , it's structured." Using examples from history and your community, outline practical steps for building structures of freedom (economic, political, or cultural) for the next generation.

WORKS CITED

Chapter 1

Ardouin, Beaubrun. *Études sur l'histoire d'Haïti: Suivies de la vie du général J.-M. Borgella.* Vol. 1, Dézobry et E. Magdeleine, 1853. *Internet Archive*, archive.org/details/etudessurlhistoi01ardo. Accessed 9 June 2026.

Berlin, Ira. *Many Thousands Gone: The First Two Centuries of Slavery in North America.* Harvard UP, 1998.

Carretta, Vincent, and Philip Gould, editors. *Genius in Bondage: Literature of the Early Black Atlantic.* UP of Kentucky, 2001.

Du Bois, W. E. B. *Black Reconstruction in America, 1860-1880.* Harcourt, Brace, 1935.

Foner, Eric. *Reconstruction: America's Unfinished Revolution, 1863-1877.* Harper and Row, 1988.

Genovese, Eugene D. *Roll, Jordan, Roll: The World the Slaves Made.* Pantheon Books, 1974.

Higman, B. W. *Slave Populations of the British Caribbean, 1807-1834.* Macmillan Caribbean, 1984.

Morgan, Philip D. *Slave Counterpoint: Black Culture in the Eighteenth-Century Chesapeake and Lowcountry.* U of North Carolina P, 1998.

National Park Service. "Gullah Geechee Cultural Heritage Corridor." *National Park Service*, www.nps.gov/places/gullah-geechee-cultural-heritage-corridor.htm. Accessed 9 June 2026.

Patterson, Orlando. *Slavery and Social Death: A Comparative Study.* Harvard UP, 1982.

Redkey, Edwin S., editor. *A Grand Army of Black Men: Letters from African American Soldiers in the Union Army, 1861-1865.* Cambridge UP, 1992.

Stuckey, Sterling. *Slave Culture: Nationalist Theory and the Foundations of Black America.* Oxford UP, 1987.

Turner, Lorenzo Dow. *Africanisms in the Gullah Dialect.* U of Chicago P, 1949.

Wood, Peter H. *Black Majority: Negroes in Colonial South Carolina from 1670 through the Stono Rebellion.* Knopf, 1974.

Chapter 2

Berlin, Ira. *Many Thousands Gone: The First Two Centuries of Slavery in North America*. Harvard UP, 1998.

Carretta, Vincent, and Philip Gould, editors. *Genius in Bondage: Literature of the Early Black Atlantic*. UP of Kentucky, 2001.

Coclanis, Peter A. *The Shadow of a Dream: Economic Life and Death in the South Carolina Low Country, 1670-1920*. Oxford UP, 1989.

Foner, Eric. *Reconstruction: America's Unfinished Revolution, 1863-1877*. Harper and Row, 1988.

Genovese, Eugene D. *Roll, Jordan, Roll: The World the Slaves Made*. Pantheon Books, 1974.

Higman, B. W. *Slave Populations of the British Caribbean, 1807-1834*. Macmillan Caribbean, 1984.

Morgan, Philip D. *Slave Counterpoint: Black Culture in the Eighteenth-Century Chesapeake and Lowcountry*. U of North Carolina P, 1998.

National Park Service. "Gullah Geechee Cultural Heritage Corridor." *National Park Service*, www.nps.gov/places/gullah-geechee-cultural-heritage-corridor.htm. Accessed 9 June 2026.

Patterson, Orlando. *Slavery and Social Death: A Comparative Study*. Harvard UP, 1982.

Wood, Peter H. *Black Majority: Negroes in Colonial South Carolina from 1670 through the Stono Rebellion*. Knopf, 1974.

Chapter 3

Beckles, Hilary McD. *A History of Barbados: From Amerindian Settlement to Nation-State.* Cambridge UP, 1990.

Blackburn, Robin. *The Making of New World Slavery: From the Baroque to the Modern, 1492-1800.* Verso, 1997.

Dubois, Laurent. *Avengers of the New World: The Story of the Haitian Revolution.* Harvard UP, 2004.

Fick, Carolyn E. *The Making of Haiti: The Saint Domingue Revolution from Below.* U of Tennessee P, 1990.

Geggus, David Patrick. *Haitian Revolutionary Studies.* Indiana UP, 2002.

Higman, B. W. *Slave Populations of the British Caribbean, 1807-1834.* Macmillan Caribbean, 1984.

James, C. L. R. *The Black Jacobins: Toussaint L'Ouverture and the San Domingo Revolution.* 2nd ed., Vintage Books, 1963.

Johnson, Howard. *The Bahamas from Slavery to Servitude, 1783-1933.* UP of Florida, 1996.

Mintz, Sidney W. *Sweetness and Power: The Place of Sugar in Modern History.* Viking, 1985.

Morgan, Philip D. *Slave Counterpoint: Black Culture in the Eighteenth-Century Chesapeake and Lowcountry.* U of North Carolina P, 1998.

Patterson, Orlando. *Slavery and Social Death: A Comparative Study.* Harvard UP, 1982.

Trouillot, Michel-Rolph. *Silencing the Past: Power and the Production of History.* Beacon Press, 1995.

Williams, Eric. *Capitalism and Slavery.* U of North Carolina P, 1944.

Chapter 4

Berlin, Ira. *Many Thousands Gone: The First Two Centuries of Slavery in North America*. Harvard UP, 1998.

Craton, Michael. *A History of the Bahamas*. Collins, 1986.

Morgan, Philip D. *Slave Counterpoint: Black Culture in the Eighteenth-Century Chesapeake and Lowcountry*. U of North Carolina P, 1998.

National Park Service. "Gullah Geechee Cultural Heritage Corridor." *National Park Service*, www.nps.gov/places/gullah-geechee-cultural-heritage-corridor.htm. Accessed 9 June 2026.

Opie, Frederick Douglass. *Hog and Hominy: Soul Food from Africa to America*. Columbia UP, 2008.

Patterson, Orlando. *Slavery and Social Death: A Comparative Study*. Harvard UP, 1982.

Saunders, Gail. *Bahamian Loyalists and Their Slaves*. Macmillan Caribbean, 1983.

Turner, Lorenzo Dow. *Africanisms in the Gullah Dialect*. U of Chicago P, 1949.

Wood, Peter H. *Black Majority: Negroes in Colonial South Carolina from 1670 through the Stono Rebellion*. Knopf, 1974.

Chapter 5

Berlin, Ira. *Many Thousands Gone: The First Two Centuries of Slavery in North America*. Harvard UP, 1998.

Du Bois, W. E. B. *Black Reconstruction in America, 1860-1880*. Harcourt, Brace, 1935.

Foner, Eric. *Reconstruction: America's Unfinished Revolution, 1863-1877*. Harper and Row, 1988.

Geggus, David Patrick. *Haitian Revolutionary Studies*. Indiana UP, 2002.

Heuman, Gad, and James Walvin, editors. *The Slavery Reader*. Routledge, 2003.

Higman, B. W. *Slave Populations of the British Caribbean, 1807-1834*. Macmillan Caribbean, 1984.

Holt, Thomas C. *The Problem of Freedom: Race, Labor, and Politics in Jamaica and Britain, 1832-1938*. Johns Hopkins UP, 1992.

James, C. L. R. *The Black Jacobins: Toussaint L'Ouverture and the San Domingo Revolution*. 2nd ed., Vintage Books, 1963.

Johnson, Howard. *The Bahamas from Slavery to Servitude, 1783-1933*. UP of Florida, 1996.

Litwack, Leon F. *Been in the Storm So Long: The Aftermath of Slavery*. Knopf, 1979.

Trouillot, Michel-Rolph. *Silencing the Past: Power and the Production of History*. Beacon Press, 1995.

Williams, Eric. *Capitalism and Slavery*. U of North Carolina P, 1944.

Chapter 6

Beckles, Hilary McD. *A History of Barbados: From Amerindian Settlement to Nation-State*. Cambridge UP, 1990.

Berlin, Ira. *Many Thousands Gone: The First Two Centuries of Slavery in North America*. Harvard UP, 1998.

Du Bois, W. E. B. *Black Reconstruction in America, 1860-1880*. Harcourt, Brace, 1935.

Foner, Eric. *Reconstruction: America's Unfinished Revolution, 1863-1877*. Harper and Row, 1988.

Geggus, David Patrick. *Haitian Revolutionary Studies*. Indiana UP, 2002.

Heuman, Gad, and James Walvin, editors. *The Slavery Reader*. Routledge, 2003.

Higman, B. W. *Slave Populations of the British Caribbean, 1807-1834*. Macmillan Caribbean, 1984.

Holt, Thomas C. *The Problem of Freedom: Race, Labor, and Politics in Jamaica and Britain, 1832-1938*. Johns Hopkins UP, 1992.

James, C. L. R. *The Black Jacobins: Toussaint L'Ouverture and the San Domingo Revolution*. 2nd ed., Vintage Books, 1963.

Johnson, Howard. *The Bahamas from Slavery to Servitude, 1783-1933*. UP of Florida, 1996.

Look Lai, Walton. *Indentured Labor, Caribbean Sugar: Chinese and Indian Migrants to the British West Indies, 1838-1918*. Johns Hopkins UP, 1993.

Mintz, Sidney W. *Sweetness and Power: The Place of Sugar in Modern History*. Viking, 1985.

Trouillot, Michel-Rolph. *Silencing the Past: Power and the Production of History*. Beacon Press, 1995.

Williams, Eric. *Capitalism and Slavery*. U of North Carolina P, 1944.

Chapter 7

Berlin, Ira. *Many Thousands Gone: The First Two Centuries of Slavery in North America.* Harvard UP, 1998.

Foner, Eric. *Give Me Liberty!: An American History*. W. W. Norton, 2011.

Gregory, James N. *The Southern Diaspora: How the Great Migrations of Black and White Southerners Transformed America*. U of North Carolina P, 2005.

Higman, B. W. *Slave Populations of the British Caribbean, 1807-1834*. Macmillan Caribbean, 1984.

James, Winston, and Clive Harris, editors. *Inside Babylon: The Caribbean Diaspora in Britain*. Verso, 1993.

Johnson, Howard. *The Bahamas from Slavery to Servitude, 1783-1933*. UP of Florida, 1996.

Look Lai, Walton. *Indentured Labor, Caribbean Sugar: Chinese and Indian Migrants to the British West Indies, 1838-1918*. Johns Hopkins UP, 1993.

Phillips, Ulrich Bonnell. *Life and Labor in the Old South*. Little, Brown, 1929.

Trouillot, Michel-Rolph. *Silencing the Past: Power and the Production of History*. Beacon Press, 1995.

Wilkerson, Isabel. *The Warmth of Other Suns: The Epic Story of America's Great Migration*. Random House, 2010.

Williams, Eric. *Capitalism and Slavery*. U of North Carolina P, 1944.

Chapter 8

Berlin, Ira. *Many Thousands Gone: The First Two Centuries of Slavery in North America.* Harvard UP, 1998.

Foner, Eric. *Give Me Liberty!: An American History.* W. W. Norton, 2011.

Johnson, Howard. *The Bahamas from Slavery to Servitude, 1783-1933.* UP of Florida, 1996.

Katz, Lawrence F., and Alan B. Krueger. "The Rise and Nature of Alternative Work Arrangements in the United States, 1995-2015." *ILR Review*, vol. 72, no. 2, 2019, pp. 382-416. doi.org/10.1177/0019793918820008.

Mintz, Sidney W. *Sweetness and Power: The Place of Sugar in Modern History.* Viking, 1985.

National Equity Atlas. "Racial Wealth Gap." *National Equity Atlas*, nationalequityatlas.org/indicators/Racial_wealth_gap. Accessed 9 June 2026.

Trouillot, Michel-Rolph. *Silencing the Past: Power and the Production of History.* Beacon Press, 1995.

U.S. Bureau of Labor Statistics. "A New Measure of Multiple Jobholding in the U.S. Economy." *Monthly Labor Review*, 2021, www.bls.gov/opub/mlr/2021/article/a-new-measure-of-multiple-jobholding-in-the-us-economy.htm. Accessed 9 June 2026.

Williams, Eric. *Capitalism and Slavery.* U of North Carolina P, 1944.

World Bank. *Latin America and the Caribbean Economic Review, October 2023: Wired--Digital Connectivity for Inclusion and Growth.* World Bank, 2023, doi.org/10.1596/978-1-4648-2038-0.

Chapter 9

Foner, Eric. *Give Me Liberty!: An American History*. W. W. Norton, 2011.

Johnson, Howard. *The Bahamas from Slavery to Servitude, 1783-1933*. UP of Florida, 1996.

Magesh, Sarath, et al. "Disparities in COVID-19 Outcomes by Race, Ethnicity, and Socioeconomic Status: A Systematic Review and Meta-analysis." *JAMA Network Open*, vol. 4, no. 11, 2021, e2134147. doi.org/10.1001/jamanetworkopen.2021.34147.

Mintz, Sidney W. *Sweetness and Power: The Place of Sugar in Modern History*. Viking, 1985.

Mujica, Oscar J., et al. "Health Inequity Focus in Pandemic Preparedness and Response Plans." *Bulletin of the World Health Organization*, vol. 100, no. 2, 2022, pp. 91-91A. doi.org/10.2471/BLT.21.287580.

National Equity Atlas. "Essential Workers." *National Equity Atlas*, nationalequityatlas.org/research/essential-workers. Accessed 9 June 2026.

Trouillot, Michel-Rolph. *Silencing the Past: Power and the Production of History*. Beacon Press, 1995.

Williams, Eric. *Capitalism and Slavery*. U of North Carolina P, 1944.

Chapter 10

Caribbean Development Dynamics 2025. Inter-American Development Bank, 2025, publications.iadb.org/en/caribbean-development-dynamics-2025. Accessed 9 June 2026.

Di Giorgio, Laura, et al. *Exploiting the Brain Gain Potential for Better Human Capital Outcomes in Belize*. KNOMAD Paper 65, World Bank, Aug. 2024, documents1.worldbank.org/curated/en/099824101032522657/pdf/IDU-fe083623-4e06-4a65-843f-8e26e34c2be8.pdf. Accessed 9 June 2026.

Girvan, Norman. *Towards a Single Development Vision and the Role of the Single Economy*. Caribbean Community Secretariat, 2006.

Johnson, Howard. *The Bahamas from Slavery to Servitude, 1783-1933*. UP of Florida, 1996.

Klak, Thomas, editor. *Globalization and Neoliberalism: The Caribbean Context*. Rowman and Littlefield, 1998.

Mintz, Sidney W. *Sweetness and Power: The Place of Sugar in Modern History*. Viking, 1985.

Trouillot, Michel-Rolph. *Silencing the Past: Power and the Production of History*. Beacon Press, 1995.

Williams, Eric. *Capitalism and Slavery*. U of North Carolina P, 1944.

World Bank. *Rethinking Caribbean Tourism: Strategies for a More Sustainable Future*. World Bank, 2025, documents.worldbank.org/en/publication/documents-reports/documentdetail/099032425104521240. Accessed 9 June 2026.

Chapter 11

Geronimus, Arline T. "The Weathering Hypothesis and the Health of African-American Women and Infants: Evidence and Speculations." *Ethnicity and Disease*, vol. 2, no. 3, 1992, pp. 207-221.

Higman, B. W. *Slave Populations of the British Caribbean, 1807-1834*. Macmillan Caribbean, 1984.

Johnson, Howard. *The Bahamas from Slavery to Servitude, 1783-1933*. UP of Florida, 1996.

Jones, Camara Phyllis. "Levels of Racism: A Theoretic Framework and a Gardener's Tale." *American Journal of Public Health*, vol. 90, no. 8, 2000, pp. 1212-1215. doi.org/10.2105/AJPH.90.8.1212.

Mintz, Sidney W. *Sweetness and Power: The Place of Sugar in Modern History*. Viking, 1985.

Pan American Health Organization. "Health Equity." *PAHO/WHO*, www.paho.org/en/topics/health-equity. Accessed 9 June 2026.

Town, Machell, et al. "Racial and Ethnic Differences in Social Determinants of Health and Health-Related Social Needs among Adults--Behavioral Risk Factor Surveillance System, United States, 2022." *Morbidity and Mortality Weekly Report*, vol. 73, no. 9, 2024, www.cdc.gov/mmwr/volumes/73/wr/mm7309a3.htm. Accessed 9 June 2026.

Trouillot, Michel-Rolph. *Silencing the Past: Power and the Production of History*. Beacon Press, 1995.

Williams, David R., and Selina A. Mohammed. "Discrimination and Racial Disparities in Health: Evidence and Needed Research." *Journal of Behavioral Medicine*, vol. 32, no. 1, 2009, pp. 20-47. doi.org/10.1007/s10865-008-9185-0.

Williams, Eric. *Capitalism and Slavery*. U of North Carolina P, 1944.

Chapter 12

Cone, James H. *A Black Theology of Liberation*. J. B. Lippincott, 1970.

Hersey, Tricia. *Rest Is Resistance: A Manifesto*. Little, Brown Spark, 2022.

Hersey, Tricia. *We Will Rest!: The Art of Escape*. Little, Brown Spark, 2025.

Higman, B. W. *Slave Populations of the British Caribbean, 1807-1834*. Macmillan Caribbean, 1984.

Johnson, Howard. *The Bahamas from Slavery to Servitude, 1783-1933*. UP of Florida, 1996.

Mintz, Sidney W. *Sweetness and Power: The Place of Sugar in Modern History*. Viking, 1985.

Trouillot, Michel-Rolph. *Silencing the Past: Power and the Production of History*. Beacon Press, 1995.

Turner, Lorenzo Dow. *Africanisms in the Gullah Dialect*. U of Chicago P, 1949.

Williams, Eric. *Capitalism and Slavery*. U of North Carolina P, 1944.

Womanist Theology. "Resources." *Womanist Theology*, www.womanisttheology.com/resources. Accessed 9 June 2026.

Chapter 13

Anderson, Claud. *PowerNomics: The National Plan to Empower Black America.* PowerNomics Corporation of America, 2001.

Davis, Angela Y. *Freedom Is a Constant Struggle: Ferguson, Palestine, and the Foundations of a Movement.* Edited by Frank Barat, Haymarket Books, 2016.

Du Bois, W. E. B. *Black Reconstruction in America, 1860-1880.* Harcourt, Brace, 1935.

Foner, Eric. *Reconstruction: America's Unfinished Revolution, 1863-1877.* Harper and Row, 1988.

Johnson, Howard. *The Bahamas from Slavery to Servitude, 1783-1933.* UP of Florida, 1996.

Mintz, Sidney W. *Sweetness and Power: The Place of Sugar in Modern History.* Viking, 1985.

Trouillot, Michel-Rolph. *Silencing the Past: Power and the Production of History.* Beacon Press, 1995.

U.S. Bureau of Labor Statistics. *Labor Force Characteristics by Race and Ethnicity, 2022.* U.S. Department of Labor, 2023, www.bls.gov/opub/reports/race-and-ethnicity/2022/. Accessed 9 June 2026.

U.S. Department of Agriculture, National Agricultural Statistics Service. *2022 Census of Agriculture: United States Summary and State Data.* Vol. 1, Geographic Area Series, pt. 51, USDA, 2024, www.nass.usda.gov/Publications/AgCensus/2022/. Accessed 9 June 2026.

World Bank. *Haiti Agriculture Sector Review.* World Bank, 2018, documents.worldbank.org/en/publication/documents-reports/documentdetail/659431538401314352/haiti-agriculture-sector-review. Accessed 9 June 2026.

Chapter 14

Anderson, Claud. *PowerNomics: The National Plan to Empower Black America.* PowerNomics Corporation of America, 2001.

Beckles, Hilary McD. *A History of Barbados: From Amerindian Settlement to Nation-State.* Cambridge UP, 1990.

Du Bois, W. E. B. *Black Reconstruction in America, 1860-1880.* Harcourt, Brace, 1935.

Foner, Eric. *Reconstruction: America's Unfinished Revolution, 1863-1877.* Harper and Row, 1988.

Girvan, Norman. *Towards a Single Development Vision and the Role of the Single Economy.* Caribbean Community Secretariat, 2006.

Higman, B. W. *Slave Populations of the British Caribbean, 1807-1834.* Macmillan Caribbean, 1984.

Holt, Thomas C. *The Problem of Freedom: Race, Labor, and Politics in Jamaica and Britain, 1832-1938.* Johns Hopkins UP, 1992.

Johnson, Howard. *The Bahamas from Slavery to Servitude, 1783-1933.* UP of Florida, 1996.

Klak, Thomas, editor. *Globalization and Neoliberalism: The Caribbean Context.* Rowman and Littlefield, 1998.

Mintz, Sidney W. *Sweetness and Power: The Place of Sugar in Modern History.* Viking, 1985.

Trouillot, Michel-Rolph. *Silencing the Past: Power and the Production of History.* Beacon Press, 1995.

Williams, Eric. *Capitalism and Slavery.* U of North Carolina P, 1944.

World Bank. "Migration and Remittances Data." *World Bank,* www.worldbank.org/en/topic/migrationremittancesdiasporaissues/brief/migration-remittance-data. Accessed 9 June 2026.

Chapter 15

Anderson, Claud. *PowerNomics: The National Plan to Empower Black America.* PowerNomics Corporation of America, 2001.

Beckles, Hilary McD. *A History of Barbados: From Amerindian Settlement to Nation-State.* Cambridge UP, 1990.

Du Bois, W. E. B. *Black Reconstruction in America, 1860-1880.* Harcourt, Brace, 1935.

Foner, Eric. *Reconstruction: America's Unfinished Revolution, 1863-1877.* Harper and Row, 1988.

Hersey, Tricia. *Rest Is Resistance: A Manifesto.* Little, Brown Spark, 2022.

Higman, B. W. *Slave Populations of the British Caribbean, 1807-1834.* Macmillan Caribbean, 1984.

Johnson, Howard. *The Bahamas from Slavery to Servitude, 1783-1933.* UP of Florida, 1996.

Klak, Thomas, editor. *Globalization and Neoliberalism: The Caribbean Context.* Rowman and Littlefield, 1998.

Mintz, Sidney W. *Sweetness and Power: The Place of Sugar in Modern History.* Viking, 1985.

Trouillot, Michel-Rolph. *Silencing the Past: Power and the Production of History.* Beacon Press, 1995.

U.S. Department of Agriculture, National Agricultural Statistics Service. *2022 Census of Agriculture: United States Summary and State Data.* Vol. 1, Geographic Area Series, pt. 51, USDA, 2024, www.nass.usda.gov/Publications/AgCensus/2022/. Accessed 9 June 2026.

Williams, Eric. *Capitalism and Slavery.* U of North Carolina P, 1944.

World Bank. "Personal Remittances, Received (% of GDP)--Caribbean Small States." *World Bank Open Data*, data.worldbank.org/indicator/BX.TRF.PWKR.DT.GD.ZS?locations=S3. Accessed 9 June 2026.

INDEX

A

B

C

D

E

F

G

H

I

J

L

M

N

O

P

R

S

T

U

W

Y

OTHER BOOKS BY CASSIUS STUART

Success The total Package
English Version
979-8-218-16590-1

A New Start in Business
English Version
978-0-57849197-4

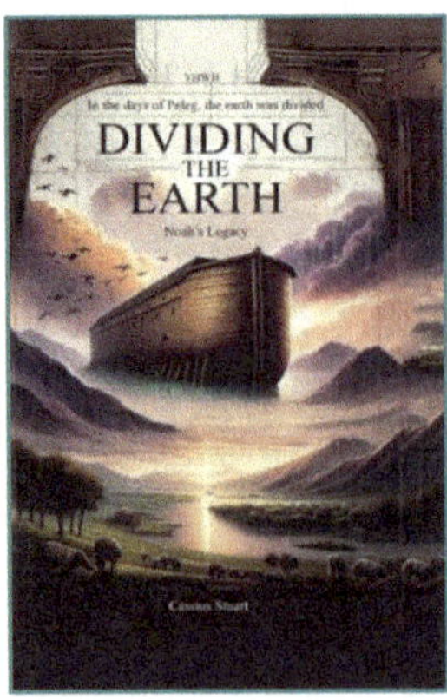

Dividing The Earth
English Version
979-8-989-63680-8

Syiera, The Dragon Slayer
English Version
979-8-989-63681-5

Raquell, A tale of Magic & Might
English Version
979-98963682-2

When the Freedom Fighters Become the Slave Masters
English Version
979-8-9896368-5-3

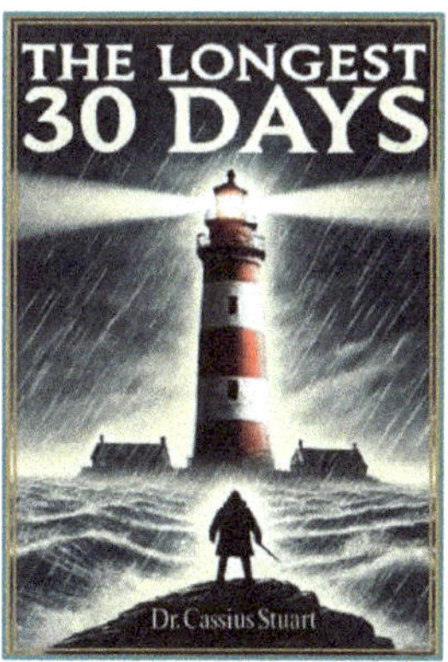

Syiera, The Dragon Slayer
English Version
979-8-989-63681-5

www.ingramcontent.com/pod-product-compliance
Lightning Source LLC
LaVergne TN
LVHW081316110826
845149LV00006B/1522
* 9 7 9 8 9 8 9 6 3 6 8 7 7 *